And DEATH WALKS with Them

Above Eight Thousand Metres with Pakistani Porters from Shimshal

CHRISTIANE FLADT

And DEATH WALKS with Them

Above Eight Thousand Metres with Pakistani Porters from Shimshal

CELEBRATING
70 YEARS OF PAKISTAN

THE **PLATINUM** SERIES

OXFORD
UNIVERSITY PRESS

OXFORD
UNIVERSITY PRESS

Oxford University Press is a department of the University of Oxford.
It furthers the University's objective of excellence in research, scholarship,
and education by publishing worldwide. Oxford is a registered trade mark of
Oxford University Press in the UK and in certain other countries

Published in Pakistan by
Ameena Saiyid, Oxford University Press
No.38, Sector 15, Korangi Industrial Area,
PO Box 8214, Karachi-74900, Pakistan

ISBN 978-0-19-940738-5

Printed on 80gsm Local Offset Paper

Printed by The Times Press Pvt. Ltd., Karachi

Contents

Introduction

'They deserve recognition.'

I HAVE THOUGHT THIS AT SEVERAL SUCH INSTANCES WHERE Shimshal's high-altitude porters and climbers were discussed, or whenever one of them returned from K-2, Nanga Parbat, or any other of the five eight-thousand-metre peaks based in Pakistan.

They deserve adequate recognition because they are not meant to lead obscure lives. Most of them are poorly paid mercenaries; two are soldiers to whom homage was sparingly paid, and there are a few genuine pioneers, but who on earth has ever heard of these unrewarded heroes?

The Sherpas in Nepal who do the same job have long before emerged from anonymity. They do not have to sell their effort and labour below a reasonable value anymore. They have scaled the social ladder and are now living in prosperity. This is also because the world's highest mountain, Mount Everest,[1] lies in Nepal. Being considered an 'easy climb', Everest is sought after by thousands of climbers who hire Sherpas to help them reach the summit.

Hardly ever does the world get to learn about their Pakistani equivalents, nor has anyone ever heard that a remarkable number of them come from Shimshal—a remote village far from K-2 and its fellow eight-thousand-metre peaks. They deserve recognition too.

After I had published three books about this village, I decided to write the fourth one about those very climbers and high-altitude porters. A logical, a necessary step, was what I thought and expected, a thrilling subject which I merely had to find out about and write down. But also a subject that would soon turn out to have its hidden and unforeseen problems.

One question which immediately surfaced concerned the selection of interviewees for this book. In Shimshal, almost all adult men will tell you that they are climbers and this is not a lie. However, the criterion for the selection of interviewees was something that baffled me for a while. A satisfactory answer to this question seemed impossible because every criterion considered had its own deficiencies.

Should the focus exclusively be on the climbers of eight-thousand-metre peaks? Among mountain enthusiasts, eight-thousand-metre peaks have become a benchmark. However, a number of seven-thousand-metre peaks, such as Dastaghil Sar (7,885 m) or Rakaposhi (7,788 m), are technically far more challenging climbs than, say, Broad Peak or Gasherbrum-II. Moreover, wouldn't it be somehow unimaginative to succumb to the 'eight-thousander'[2] hype, which exists for merely one reason: the triumph of the metric system?

Another guiding principle could be the total number of a climber's expeditions—the more, the better; or rather, the number of summits climbed successfully? However, even in this case, one does not surely know where to draw the line, or how to define the limit below which a HAP cannot belong to the selected few. Is it even fair to consider HAPs based on the 'minimum number' of peaks they have successfully ascended?

It is quite clear that no strict criteria can be applied to measure the 'competence' and 'success' of HAPs because they are mostly at the mercy of weather. The god of weather favours both the amateur and the expert, and surely makes the master fail no less miserably than the beginner.

Since I did not wish to proceed in a purely arbitrary manner, my guiding principle for the selection of interviewees had been the 'eight-thousander-method'. Whoever has stood on the summit of at least one of Pakistan's five eight-thousand-metre peaks[3] was interviewed and is represented in the book.

There are further reasons why this book project happened to be less than simple. I had expected that the subject of climbing expeditions, the figure of the high altitude porter, and the setting of the eight-thousanders would inherently provide suspense and drama. This was unfortunately a misconception.

I had anticipated that Shimshalis' tales would brim with avalanches, gaping crevasses, tattered tents, and Westerners suffering from high-altitude sickness on Nanga Parbat's Diamir Wall or at K-2's Bottleneck. This wasn't the case, however. Quite a few of my climbers, when asked about their expeditions, could only remember cursory details. Time and again, I urged them to recall details such as the leader's or the members' conduct, the preparation of tea at thousands of metres above sea level, and the nights spent in storm-rattled and snow-covered tents. All efforts towards this end went futile. Some HAPs could only shrug their shoulders, which made me think if it was even possible for them to forget everything. Is high-portering just a job, or a routine which does not deserve to be remembered? Or does this also have to do with the Shimshalis' profoundly different attitude towards time, towards the past, the present, and the future?

I must mention here that what counts in Shimshal is the present moment. Life is here and now, and everything else is secondary and arbitrary. Confusing 'yesterday' and 'tomorrow' is a popular error. Dates and years are totally unimportant; many do not even know how old they are or when they were married. The future is a vague terrain anyway. Plans, appointments, and meetings are located in thin air at best. Plans will hardly aim further than tonight or tomorrow, and 'tomorrow' is also likely to mean 'the day after tomorrow' or just 'later'.

However, there are a number of significant exceptions among my interviewees. Amin Ullah Baig, Aziz Baig, Hazil Shah, and Ali Musa related exciting stories of their own accord. Similarly, Rajab Shah and Meherban Shah—the two senior figures among the eight-thousander climbers—gave me insights from the wealth of their memories, although these memories had been partly wiped out through twin horrors: both lost their eldest sons in climbing accidents within two years. This affliction virtually buried portions of their recollections.

I complete my list of problems with the trickiest one: the issue of truth. Generally hunters and sailors are known to mix fact and fiction, and by any account, so are climbers. For instance, in his new book *Back to Tomorrow* (*Zurück nach Morgen*, Malik 2012), Hans Kammerlander writes about many fabrications among mountaineers. He decries in strong words how selfishness and craving for stardom rule in the climbing community. He concludes that more often than not, everything falls victim to personal success and so does the truth. On p. 246 of his book, he writes: 'Today I believe that lying and romancing have become the commonest thing on the slopes of the eight-thousanders.'

This judgement is aimed at his Western climbing colleagues but similar fabrications are being traded among Pakistanis and thus among Shimshalis also.

The question then is if it is even worthwhile to read this book in view of such uncertainties and imponderables?

To read or not to read is the reader's prerogative; however, writing the book was worth the effort. During my interviews I became acquainted with the most manifold faces, characters, and biographies of 'my' climbers, not to ignore their families and homes. Along with my interpreter, Samad Karim, I walked distances of up to 16 kilometres to interview them. Without exception, we were offered tea and 'shapik'[4] during our conversations, and received cordial words of gratitude while parting from them. It made them glad to see that their achievements were appreciated and valued.

These achievements are definitely magnificent. I have had my own experiences on expeditions although on a small scale. They enable me to appraise the amount of strength, skilfulness, doggedness, readiness to suffer, and defiance of death that a high-altitude porter has to afford. I admire and salute them.

The fact that high-portering is a job which generates money does not diminish the magnitude of their exploits. This book's object and aspiration is to pay homage to these men and introduce them as individuals and personalities to mountain lovers and climbing enthusiasts.[5]

The title of the book is a quote from Lal Paree whose husband Qudrat Ali used to work as a high-altitude porter and mountain guide, and spent every summer from 1998 to 2008 in the so-called Death Zone.[6] When Lal described her anxieties about her husband, the image appearing in her inner eye was of a vulnerable human creature stepping in waist-high snow, 'and death was walking with him'.

Notes

1. Everest's summit is crossed by the Nepalese-Chinese border but the majority of climbs are carried out from the Nepalese side.
2. 'Eight-thousander' is a common term in the mountaineers' jargon. It is used to describe fourteen independent mountains on earth that are more than 8,000 metres high above sea level.
3. The other nine 8,000-metre peaks in Nepal and China are hardly within the Shimshalis' reach.
4. The local pita bread and everything that is made of flour and water.
5. The high-altitude porters of Hunza and Baltistan are by no means inferior to the Shimshalis. However, since my scope of action and my background knowledge is restricted to Shimshal, and the book as such must not overstep a given frame, I request the reader to see the Shimshali high-altitude porters as deputies of their Hunza and Balti colleagues.
6. A term used by mountain climbers to refer to high-altitude zones where there is not enough oxygen for humans to breathe. This is usually eight-thousand metres above sea level.

Section One

People and the Landscape of Shimshal

1.1

Shimshal: The Village

IT WAS IN THE YEAR 2002 THAT I FIRST SET FOOT IN SHIMSHAL. Since that time, I have been observing and recording the village's development during my annual sojourns of several months or even years.

Shimshal lies in the Pakistani region of Gilgit-Baltistan, i.e. in the outermost north-east of the country, and on the edge of the Karakoram Mountains. It is surrounded by five- and six-thousand metre high peaks and is not far from the seven-thousand metre peaks Dastaghil Sar and Yukshin Gardan. Similarly, Pakistan's eight-thousand metre peaks are no more than 120 kilometres away as the crow flies.

The village is situated at exactly 3,000 metres above sea level. Its individual settlements Farmanabad, Aminabad, Centre Shimshal, and Khizerabad spread along approximately nine kilometres in the Shimshal Valley. Estimates of the population have ranged from 1,700 to 2,000 people since the year 2003. A census has never really been performed so no one knows the population figures precisely. However, the number of yaks, also the pride of every Shimshali, is common knowledge. They are about 1,400 in total. These sure-footed, shaggy, and traditional cattle live only sporadically and temporarily down in the village, i.e. when they serve as means of transport from and to the high pastures. Their proper habitats are generally above 4,000 metres; they graze at just under 5,000 metres and spend the winter beyond the passes at around 3,500 metres.

The Shimshalis, almost untouched by the outside world, maintained the archaic lifestyle of shepherds and farmers until a short time ago because the village could only be reached after days of arduous walking. This remoteness made the inhabitants self-sustaining. It was a cause for pride, but increasingly also for frustration and anger at being more or less ignored and forgotten by the government in Islamabad.

However, since the opening of a 55-km-long jeepable road (which had largely been built by the Shimshalis themselves, more often than not at the risk of their lives), the village has seen significant progress. Ever since, it has experienced at a frantic pace what the Europeans have been able to process and digest quietly in the course of a hundred years.

Almost unanimously, the Shimshalis perceive the changes of the past ten years as a blessing. In addition to their passengers, the four jeep owners carry the new age to Shimshal in the form of plastic tubes, diesel generators, foam mattresses, solar panels, toilet bowls, TV sets, and a lot more. The goods that arrive in the village are well-packaged and tied up on the vehicles' roofs.

The youngsters, on the one hand, cannot use their cell-phones which they brought from the provincial capital Gilgit or from the cities of Islamabad and Karachi because the village, trapped among jagged peaks, is cut off from mobile phone service. However, they have recorded hundreds of songs, local and/or religious music predominantly, which they play at any occasion. Miraculously, charging the cell phone is easier in Shimshal than in the rest of Pakistan which suffers from chronic load-shedding. The tiny hydropower station in

Aminabad does its service in a more reliable manner than those in Hunza or Islamabad. The water power station is operational from May to October, that is as long as the river flows from the Adver Sar Glacier.

The youngsters of Shimshal are away from the village nowadays. However, this is not only due to the well-known gravitational pull that cities and metropolises exert across the world. There is simultaneously the urge and obligation to get higher education. In this village we witness with both pleasure and concern the two faces of education: a blessing and a curse.

Being Ismailis, the Shimshalis staunchly adhere to their *Weltanschauung* and principles of their spiritual leader, His Highness Prince Karim Aga Khan, on whose red and green flags education is invisibly but insistently propagated as one of the highest values. The first school in Shimshal was built in the late sixties of the twentieth century. Today there are three, and you will hardly find a single child who will not attend school, although school uniforms, textbooks, and monthly fees cost the families dearly. The Shimshalis' passion for learning has had the most remarkable impact on their English. Compared with the rest of Pakistan, there is a substantial number of people over here who understand and speak English, if at varying levels. In the Hunza Valley, people say, half mockingly, half enviously, 'In Shimshal even the yaks talk in English.'

Each of the climbers I interviewed and, towards the end, quizzed about their children's future, emphasized that acquiring education was their ultimate goal.

Education enables us to advance. It is a precondition for jobs, and, last but not the least, offers the kind of life which is more enlightened and complete due to a wealth of knowledge, ideas, and wisdom. Surprisingly, these notions have arrived sustainably in the outermost village near the Chinese border. Isn't this what we have forever fancied for countries such as Pakistan?

Why then do I link the term 'curse' with the concept of education? By no means do I wish to discredit its inherent value. What I do see, however, is a dialectic which is innate in education and cannot possibly be resolved. There is evidence in Shimshal that the rise of education contributes to the erosion of traditional lifestyles. For instance, when a family has drudgingly saved money for a son's IT training, the son will be lost to Shimshal. He will need to find a well-paid job but where else other than in a big city? He will stay there, transfer money home to his family, and later send for his new wife to join him in the city. His parents might be able to abandon one or two fields and thus get rid of some of their incessant toil. The same cycle repeats with a daughter. What meaningful work, I wonder, will an educated young woman find in Shimshal? Tending the sheep and goats is out of the question. It is true that there is a need of good teachers and nurses but their number is limited and their salary low.

Moreover, both the son and daughter, after getting used to the cities' amenities and comforts, will see the meagre and exhausting life in their native village with fresh and sceptical eyes. When the sons leave, fields will be untended, and when the daughters are absent, the houses in the high pastures will remain locked—a development which has already started. The predominantly elder women who are still devoted to keeping up the traditional Pamir life are the dwindling species, and an age is announcing itself where no cheese or butter will make the journey down to Shimshal. Not only will a unique shepherding culture be buried but a precious type of food will be lost forever to be replaced with a faceless, low-grade item, and that too for too much money on top of that.

As far as money is concerned, financial considerations will also steer the Shimshalis towards the idea of abandoning a field or two. Until 1997, they threshed their crops with the support of yaks or oxen. Today there are five threshing machines, which are all owned by business-oriented individuals. Since nobody wishes any longer to endure the time-consuming travails of traditional threshing, the owners have felt free to gradually raise the threshing rates per operation to a dizzying level: 35 rupees per minute[1]! Therefore, a six-hour job, as called for by a medium-sized family, costs 22,600 rupees, which is the equivalent of what a teacher earns in a couple of months. Small wonder then that a family's breadwinner will start calculating if it is worth the effort of growing his own crops. Under close scrutiny, the white flour that one can buy in Hunza and readily tie up in sacks is less expensive. It may be true that the white flour has not proved of value lately, especially after the Attabad disaster[2] when the Chinese airlifted rice, oil, sugar, and white flour to Shimshal. The flour caused constipation and drained the strength from people's legs. Yet, modern health maxims are a luxury and beyond the Shimshalis' reach. What counts is the toil and drudgery that goes into ploughing and sowing and in many months of irrigating or in cutting (by hand and with sickles), threshing, sifting, washing, and grinding. For centuries, these tasks had determined the rhythm of daily life. These were unquestioned and never doubted, though incredibly harsh.

Today modern amenities are well-known. If more comfort costs less money, who would reproach the Shimshalis for preferring comfort?

Both the exodus of young people and the gradual disappearance of agriculture and livestock breeding have triggered a process that cannot be stopped and will result in the loss of what the villagers still proudly proclaim to be 'their culture'. I keep encountering young Shimshalis who discuss this process and vow to give shape to it and to make themselves useful in their native village. Until now, however, I have not seen a serious approach or a coordinated strategy, and hardly any precise and tangible objectives. On the one hand there are considerable numbers of boards, committees, and similar institutions in the village while on the other there is a lack of willpower, perseverance, and cooperation among them. The deeply rooted system of family clans, which firmly stick together and support their members unconditionally, is alive and kicking. Shimshalis are humans after all. They are no less subject to the sentiments of personal vanities, envy, and greed than the Europeans or Americans.

Moreover, when NGOs[3] from far-away countries interfere and urgently want to do good deeds following their own concepts, the issues become even trickier. In Shimshal, there are numerous projects financed by foreign sponsors, old and new, Canadian, Japanese, German, and those from New Zealand but few of them have exclusively been a blessing for the community. The reason has been primarily a lack of patience in the initiators who wanted to signal their sympathy and affection and went on to impulsively start their projects without any particular expertise.

The Shimshalis admit in charming openness that they are not unaware of the problems.

As it is, they like to woo those foreigners who promise a sudden flow of cash. Who would not be tempted to offer his services as a mediator, to add an aura of glory to his family, and casually benefit a little bit from this role? It is enough to just hint at the lucrative potential of engaging oneself with the

NGOs that come with the best intentions, not to mention the much-discussed question of sustainability.

There is another downside of NGOs which is rarely discussed but has to be taken seriously: they provide excuses for the Islamabad government to keep twiddling its thumbs, while it is its duty to develop infrastructure and help people out of distress.

It was a sensational piece of information, though a long desired one, when, in the summer of 2012, it was learnt that Islamabad had given the green light to a big hydropower station on the Shimshal River. It meant the availability of electricity throughout the year. Electricity not only for bulbs and chargers but also for washing machines and refrigerators! Should this long-fostered dream come true in the near future, its location is planned to be near Kuk, ca. 15 km downstream from Shimshal. It would mean a huge leap in the Shimshalis' quality of life. What is still missing is a telephone/mobile/Internet link with the outside world, but this also seems to be moving forward.

Whether these things will slow down the exodus from the community remains to be seen but they are unlikely to stem the gradual vanishing of animal husbandry and agriculture.

For more than twenty years, the Canadian ethnologist and geographer David Butz and his wife Nancy[4] have done research on Shimshal's social structure, recent development, and its prospects in the future. It is an incredibly complex and varied subject.

Even though we can observe a certain disintegration of the traditional lifestyle with the increasing pull of the big cities and the rising intractability of a number of emerging problems, Shimshal is not doomed.

This village will survive.

The Shimshalis' instinct for practical matters is strong, as is their resourcefulness and their penchant to do the right thing, even at the last possible moment.

The point here is that it is not the Western perspective that determines the right thing but the view of the Shimshalis.

Notes

1. As of September 2013.
2. On 4 January 2010, a mammoth rockslide closed off the valley of the Hunza River between Gulmit and Hunza. The dam that was formed created a lake 22 km in length, which made the KKH and countless houses, fields, and orchards disappear in its waters.
3. Non-governmental organizations, i.e. developmental charities.
4. See www.brocku.ca

1.2

The Mountain People of Shimshal

The following sections are meant to elucidate why Shimshal is a breeding ground for excellent climbers

Walking as a way of life

IN SHIMSHAL, PEOPLE MOVE SOLELY ON FOOT. THEY HAVE always done so and they still do, regardless of the jeep road to Passu. Neither do horses nor automobiles (apart from the public transport vehicles) exist in the village, and there are exactly three bicycles. One's feet are the primary means of moving around.[1]

Moving, advancing, and shifting in Shimshal almost always implies walking uphill or downhill, on steep and often rugged terrain and scree slopes, at breakneck speed, for instance when you have to retrieve a stray goat. When a Westerner sees Shimshalis sprint, he can hardly understand whether their feet touch the ground; they almost seem to dance across obstacles with a dreamlike confidence that may be called instinct.

The simple truth is that walking means surviving. In order to mend the irrigation channels in springtime, you have to walk several kilometres, run across unstable scree, and balance along vertical rocks. In order to build or fix trails, you have to cross rivers and scale passes. Shimshalis are familiar with any kind of ground. They know the treacherous debris of moraines no less than jumbles of huge rocks, and pebbles and sand no different than the glassy black ice of glaciers. They can cross rivers jumping from one rock to another, carrying a 25 kg rucksack on their back. Winter after winter, the men who spend seven months with the yaks beyond the high pastures have to struggle through snow which can be knee-, hip-, and even shoulder-deep.

Consequently, a person who possesses surefootedness, agility, and stamina just like he possesses his mother tongue will clearly benefit from those skills on the slopes of the eight-thousand-metre peaks.

Carrying loads as a way of life

Almost as early as the skill of walking becomes part of their system, Shimshalis begin to get used to carrying loads. As soon as the children start moving safely on their own legs, they haul around their baby siblings just for fun. Boys help to carry rocks for house construction; girls walk home from the spring with their backs stooped under heavy water containers.

Later in life, the people in Shimshal tie giant bundles of firewood or loads of wheat sheaves to their backs. They shift potato and barley sacks from one place to the other. There is not a single day that passes without hauling, lugging, toting.

Consequently, a person who is as deeply accustomed to carrying loads as he is to the eternal noise of the Shimshal River will not frown at his expedition leader when receiving the high-altitude porter's load of 16 kg.

Enduring cold as a way of life

High-altitude climbing means enduring extreme cold that is painful and brings tears to the eyes.

Is there any Westerner who has an idea of such cruel cold? We have built well-insulated walls and roofs between ourselves and the outside world and we sit in centrally heated rooms; or we get into an automobile which is waiting at our very front door and might even be pre-heated or wonderfully air-conditioned.

In the event that we do expose ourselves to the fresh winter breeze, we wrap our frames in several layers of down and hi-tech fibres so it is only the nose that will turn a bit red. What gives us additional comfort is the security of our permanently heated home, or at least of a pub on the way, where we can warm up with a glass of hot spiced wine.

Not so in Shimshal though.

In Shimshal, life is lived outdoors, except in the heat of summer when you have to escape from the sun. A house is rarely a place to linger, and even less a place to work. It is meant for sleeping and eating. When there are visitors, it may happen that people sit and chat for half an hour, otherwise you rise after the final sip of water and leave. Unless you are ill, you are not entitled to stay at home.

Whether indoors or outdoors, in winters, one is sure to constantly feel cold as winter is long in Shimshal: seven freezing months at the minimum. Firewood is precious and thus can only be burned when meals are being cooked. Nobody can afford to heat a stove for warmth. Such extravagance might be offered to a special guest or, exceptionally, in the schools when the classroom temperature has dropped below zero (mercifully, January is holiday time).

The practice of enduring cold starts early on in life. Whereas babies are still well packaged (often tied up in the traditional style), while being rocked in their wooden cradles, the parental care quickly lets up when the infant has gotten rid of his diapers and a new baby has occupied the cradle. Not infrequently, on cold October days, I encounter a bunch of kids playing, their lips blue with cold and their noses running with remarkable amounts of snot. They are hardly wearing more than two pieces of clothing which include a thin cotton T-shirt and an equally thin pair of pants. More often than not have I tried to appeal to mothers, sisters, and brothers about this. They did listen kindly because yes, sure I was right; the kids should definitely pull on some warm stuff. When I did not relent and asked why were they shivering in the autumn gale in their scanty gear, they looked half self-conscious, half indifferent, and claimed it was the focus on the endless work in the fields and the livestock that made them forget and neglect the children.

But adults in Shimshal do not in any way care better for their own well-being. Just like the children, mothers keep wearing their thin colourful shalwar kameez until late autumn. Heaven knows why. Perhaps for reasons of beauty. (Mera Jabeen, ca. 20 years old, told me in Shuwerth, Shimshal's high pasture at 4,600 metres, in a bitingly cold wind that she did not wish to look so *baj*, which is Shimshali equivalent of fat). Mind you, there are plenty of padded jackets in Shimshal.

Of course, all festivities are carried out in the open and many of them, especially the weddings, are scheduled in the cold season.

Consequently, a person who from early childhood has become accustomed to living outside predominantly, both in summer and winter, to doing their daily work in the open while stoically ignoring frozen limbs and chattering teeth, will remain unimpressed when at 6,200 metres in camp 2, the inside of the tent and the sleeping bag develop a thick layer of ice, or when he has to fix a rope at minus 30 degrees Celsius in gale-force winds.

Resourcefulness as a way of life

Before something is discarded in Shimshal, it has to be broken truly and irreparably. Before its irrevocable end, it is generally mended, fixed, and repaired a hundred times. Where a European will most probably fail to see any prospect and declare an object hopelessly beyond repair, a Shimshali will find some way to fix it and make sure that the pressure cooker, the battery-driven watch, or the torn backpack are again fully functional. Not only is this resourcefulness a remarkable talent and an attitude we have mostly lost in our throwaway society, in extremity it may also save lives.

If the cap of a thermos bottle is no longer watertight, a Shimshali knows the trick of stopping the leakage. When the zipper of a high-camp tent fails to close (a near catastrophe), a Shimshali will surely know how to make it work again. As I already mentioned, these mountain dwellers were catapulted into the age of hi-tech within just a few years. With their practical sense, and at breathtaking speed, they have acquired all the skills they need to utilize modern gadgets.

A person who until yesterday threshed his crops with yaks or stepped through the snow wearing socks made of goat skin, now fixes solar panels and masters all the tricks of a digital camera.

In the life-threatening, hostile world of the eight-thousand-metre peaks, where more often than not the breadth of a hair lies between life and death, such a versatile person will move with self-confidence and mental strength, which in turn he will convey to his companions and clients and thereby give them courage.

Note

1. Lately, the occasional motorbike has turned up.

1.3

Climbing: A Job or a Philosophy?

WHAT DO WE HAVE TO PICTURE WHEN THINKING OF A Shimshali climber's life? It hardly resembles the life of a Western mountaineer. Backgrounds and biographies could not be more divergent.

European, American, and Australian mountaineers are a pretty varied bunch when we consider their lifestyles, education, walks of life, and families. We find fathers and mothers as well as people without children; there are both married and single persons among them. Western climbers come from diverse professional backgrounds. You can meet a dentist, a bank clerk, a mailman, as well as a jailhouse priest, a carpenter, or a headmistress. Very few of them succeed in becoming professional climbers. To most of them, climbing is a hobby. It serves as a compensation and recreation after their workdays, which are almost exclusively spent indoors and in the stench of cities and metropolises.

The Western climbers invest a lot of money in equipment, membership dues, course fees, costs of transportation to and from the mountains, overnight stay, and so on. Some of them have the sole aim of climbing an eight-thousand-metre peak and they scrimp and save for the five-digit monetary amounts that are involved.

What Westerners also associate with mountaineering is a

notion of freedom, closeness to nature, fresh air, and physical exercise. Last but not the least, mountains represent an unspoilt, sometimes romantic, or even mystical world to them, which is conjured up in countless books, soulful songs, and sundry well-known or infamous movies.

You will hardly find such an idea among the Shimshalis.

I met the most diverse characters during my interviews but, as I expected, they did not differ in their lifestyles, save a mere two or three of them.

All of them are married and fathers of several children; some are even grandfathers.

Besides Qudrat Ali, Shaheen Baig, and Ali Musa, who visit Shimshal only sporadically, each of them is essentially a farmer, shepherd, craftsman, and occasional hunter.

Since the road opened in 2003, a few Shimshalis, including some mountaineers, have tried to launch small enterprises. Why not open a general store in a 9-square-metre room in Shimshal or Aliabad[1], or be a keen optimist and build a guesthouse for trekkers and tourists; or even establish a small one-man operation which offers tours ranging from yak safaris to the expeditions to eight-thousand-metre peaks?

These start-ups rarely get going, or they fail before long because the owners lack vision and stamina. The idea is to earn money whenever there seems to be a promising trend or an assumed demand. It was Qudrat Ali, who had a homepage made with gaudy photos and florid texts, which promises the most magnificent things to potential trekkers and climbers. The rates are substantial and do not rank behind those of the leading tour operators like ATP, Nazir Sabir Expeditions, Caravan Leaders, and Hunza Guides. Western climbers are generally considered filthy rich and this cannot even be disputed from a Pakistani point of view.

Qudrat Ali's company Shams Alpine, which he founded in 2005, can still be found on the internet but it has been mothballed because he and his friend Shaheen Baig are pursuing a more lucrative occupation. Similarly, Hazil Shah's tour operation has long since been discontinued and his tourist lodge in Shimshal is often deserted too.

To be fair, I have to add that it is also the political situation in Pakistan that has contributed to these near failures.

Even though the foreign media drafts an image of Pakistan which is regrettably biased and undifferentiated, it cannot be denied that the interests of the so-called Joe Bloggs have never really been represented by Pakistani politicians. Politics is essentially controlled by civilian bureaucrats, the army, or the established elites. There are also the religious extremists and militant groups who succeed in nipping in the bud any approach towards a functioning system.

This particularly affects a region like Gilgit-Baltistan which largely depends on mountain tourism as a source of income. Any new report of a deadly shoot-out between Sunnis and Shias will cause foreign offices to pronounce warnings and travel businesses to cancel their trips.

It is quite clear now that climbing can hardly be called a hobby in a Shimshali's life. As a job, it also occupies comparatively little time, not least because it is restricted to the months of June through August (unless you join winter expeditions like Amin Ullah Baig does, for instance). It is all the more impressive how many summits are listed in the records of several Shimshalis, as the reader will learn in this book.

In a similar way, the basics and preparations for an expedition in Shimshal are worlds apart from the prearrangements of a Westerner. Whereas the latter typically practises over weeks and months, even years, and with a strong focus, one will not even remotely come across the idea of 'training' or 'exercise' in Shimshal. When, high above the village in October 2012, I met Amin Ullah Baig, who was taking a number of yaks to the far-away high pasture of Guijerav, he laughingly named his hike 'acclimatization' (for the said winter expedition). Daily life is sufficient practise for Shimshalis; they don't feel the need to adhere to any theories, targets, and objectives.

Shimshalis are quick to grasp technical skills such as using ice axes, ropes, karabiners, and ice screws. Some of 'my' climbers learned these skills in no time at all and that too while joining their first expeditions. For the others it was Rajab Shah's two- or three-day training on the Malangutti Glacier, 15 km downstream from Shimshal, which made them fit to meet the demands of high-portering.

How do the HAPs[2] get the costly equipment that is required for their job? A Western climber who embarks on an eight-thousand-metre-peak's expedition will easily spend 3,000 to 5,000 euros on his complete equipment, depending on his standards and bank account.

Unlike the low porters, who haul the bulk of the expedition paraphernalia to base camps and often wear ripped textile or rubber shoes, thin trousers, and threadbare sweaters while hurrying along the glaciers, the HAPs have come to obtain adequate equipment from their tour operators. They get to keep the things after the expedition. This enables them to opt for cash rather than equipment on their next expedition.

At some point in June, the lone satellite phone that is stationed in Shimshal starts the season. It is the only link with the outside world and has replaced the radio as a means of communicating news to the climbers. It announces the names of those HAPs who have been selected for expeditions. ATP,[3] for one, calls for Sarwar Ali, and Nazir Sabir Expeditions calls for Aziz Baig. These Shimshalis are available at all times of the day and night. Heaven knows for how long they will be absent. The family will live in complete uncertainty from this point on, but such has always been their routine. Who would presume to forecast the weather, or a new job opportunity, let alone an accident or illness?

One fine day the father or husband will knock on the front door again, Insha'Allah. He will have done his job and made good money. With his labour and drudgery in freezing temperatures, constantly facing mortal danger, he will have succeeded in earning enough money to finance another semester or two for his son and daughter. This is what he toils for.

Should a Westerner begin to try and tell Aziz about the grandeur and loftiness of the mountains, their healing powers, and attempt to lift climbing into the dizzying spheres of philosophy, he would probably shrug his shoulders. What is he talking about? A mountain is a mountain. You climb it willy-nilly to earn money.

However, it is not all Shimshali climbers who feel they are mere mercenaries. During my interviews, some surprised me with terms that indeed overstepped this narrow perception. Qurban Mohammad, for example, professes a 'love of adventure sport'. For his part, Sarwar Ali sees climbing not least as a meaningful activity, which can be free of material purposes.

The payment of high-altitude porters is not subject to any mandatory rule in Pakistan. Each tour operator handles it at his own discretion. All HAPs seem to have reasonable insurance nowadays. When asked about their wages, Shimshalis name anything between 1,500 and 2,500 rupees per day which in

2013 was the equivalent of about 11 to 13 euros. Some claim that they feel fine with their salary; others say it is not enough. Discontent is likely to originate from comparison with the Nepalese Sherpas. For more than seventy years, the Sherpas have been 'imported' to the Karakorams from their native mountains and have been competing with the local high-altitude porters, who are dumbfounded when they learn about the enterprising Sherpas' salaries. As early as 2001, a 'star Sherpa' was able to make up to 25,000 dollars per year. Extra bonuses are given for reaching the summit of these mountains. For instance, ascending to the peak of Mount Everest could come with a high bounty of up to 5,000 dollars.

Hans Kammerlander calls the Sherpas 'high-salaried'.[4] Graham Bowley, in his 2010 book *No Way Down* which talks about the 2008 catastrophe on K-2, claims that the local HAPs are 'a cheaper alternative' to the Nepalese Sherpas.

Moritz Steinhilber, an expert on both the Karakorams and the Nepalese Himalayas, knows of Khumbu Sherpas who invested their high-porter salaries in hotels. They rented these out while they themselves are now living in Kathmandu, New Delhi, or New York as dollar millionaires.

Meanwhile, the Sherpas' prestige in their own country has also soared to heights that are unimaginable for Pakistani high-altitude porters.

Deepak Thapa, a Nepalese journalist, in his chapter for the book titled *Journey to the Himalayas*,[5] discusses the recent progress. Until about ten years ago, the Sherpas too were considered 'nameless workhorses'.[6] They showcase themselves today as experts in technical climbing who essentially combine the tasks of both high-altitude porters and mountain guides.

In Pakistan, this kind of corporate self-image is painfully missing even though the Balti, Shimshali, and Hunzakut

HAPs' work is never simply restricted to just carrying loads. They regularly prepare the route, fix ropes, support and rescue members in distress, and even risk their lives when retrieving injured climbers or dead bodies. Unfortunately, a corresponding awareness, public perception, and documentation of these efforts and exploits are deplorably poor, and altogether non-existent in some cases.

According to Ali Musa, this is to some extent the HAPs' own fault. Each of them muddles along by himself. None takes initiative to develop cooperation and infrastructure, or an umbrella organization or a trade union which might be able to shape an identity and foster some sort of solidarity.

Also, the Pakistani high-altitude porters seem to care little about being submissive. Rather, they have a reputation for being stubborn and defiant as opposed to the Sherpas who are known as compliant and deferential.

Ali Musa demands that Pakistan's Ministry of Tourism should take better care of the HAPs since they are one of the very pillars of mountain tourism. The tour operators such as Nazir Sabir, Caravan Leaders, Hunza Guides, and others could contribute to improve networking among the high porters, but he adds that they prefer to look after themselves even though they get a lot of profit from the HAPs.

In Nepal, according to Deepak Thapa, the new generation of climbers is raising their educational standards.[7]

Coming to the question of a new generation of climbers, I wonder whether such a species can be found in Shimshal. Quite paradoxically, this situation is also due to education. In order to explain the logic of my argument, I will have to expand on the topic and consider the Shimshal Mountaineering School (SMS).

It was this mountaineering school that Qudrat Ali founded

in 2009 with support from Italian Simone Moro and The North Face. He donated part of his own land and erected an elaborate and prominently placed building.

Initially, Qudrat's idea looked perfectly plausible to me. He said he wanted to disseminate his mountaineering skills, knowledge, and enthusiasm to the young generation. The fact that he conformed to Simone's wish and included girls in the programme was, in my eyes, almost revolutionary.

Some training sessions were conducted on the Malangutti and Adver Sar glaciers; indeed, a handful of highly skilled young climbers have emerged from these events. In January 2011, Qudrat even succeeded in taking the girls to the summit of Mingli Sar (6,015m) under the most gruelling conditions. This was a great accomplishment.

The SMS has a colourful homepage on the internet; however, its exuberant texts stand in strange opposition to reality. On all but a few days of the year, the SMS building stands locked and deserted. Qudrat may have had a laudable idea but he did not design a logical concept with long-term goals and intentions, a realistic strategy, and partners who will implement the project and foster cooperation in the long run. Most importantly, he no longer lives in Shimshal.

A question arises with regards to the goal of the mountaineering school. Was it established to train new high-altitude porters, registered mountain guides, or men who no longer have to suffer as workhorses? The vague phrases on the SMS homepage are hardly enlightening.

Oddly enough, Pakistan—the land of K-2 and Nanga Parbat, and other great mountains in the world—does not have a mountain guides association. Consequently, no one in Pakistan can really acquire the internationally acknowledged title of a mountain guide. If Qudrat really wants to advance things, he will have to act at the level of the Alpine Club Pakistan, as quoted from Ali Musa.

When I questioned Shimshal's long-serving high-altitude porters and climbers about the SMS, they neither openly criticized it nor showed any enthusiasm. Shimshalis are typically tight-lipped and if they do talk, it is mostly in an ironical manner; you seldom know whether they really mean it. Ali Musa thinks the school is in the wrong place. It should have been built in the Hunza Valley, or in Gilgit or Islamabad in order to attract young people from other parts of the country. According to him, the journey to Shimshal is much too arduous for people from other parts of Pakistan.

Ali Musa also does not see any prospects for female climbers. He is convinced that parents and husbands will never allow their daughters and wives to join the male world of high-altitude climbing.

The catchphrase 'gender equality' is being proudly pronounced by several young Shimshalis and the female climbers serve as evidence for their progressive mindset.

Although this is welcome and pleasing news, 'gender equality' in its full sense still remains a milestone to be achieved.

Those Westerners who expect a leap towards female emancipation will be disappointed with regard to the SMS. It is still men who take the initiative and they will continue to be in a commanding position unless a miracle happens.

The girls and women are used to the patriarchal status quo and in no way do they object to male pre-eminence. To them, it is just and right, and questioning it is beyond their wildest dreams.

It is part of what Shimshalis call their 'culture'. Apparently, it does not occur to the climbing girls to feel freer or more advanced than others, let alone pacemakers in the field of women's rights. Ali Musa is quite right when he says that the girls' expeditions are 'just for excitement'.[8] There is no dividend or a palpable profit which in his eyes is a shortcoming.

Shimshal's mountaineers see climbing as part of their identity.

Qudrat Ali and his longtime friend, Shaheen Baig—the aces among Shimshal's mountaineers—love to enthuse over the fascination of technical climbing which requires all those sophisticated jingling gadgets that are clipped to the maestros' harness. Such equipment conveys stature and, to be very frank, masculinity as well.

Qurban Mohammad regards himself not solely as a high-altitude porter but also as an adventure lover. Sarwar Ali sees value in climbing beyond making money.

On the other hand, Shimshalis are not in a position to practise climbing just for its own sake. None of them can spare the time except perhaps a youngster who takes a two- or three-day hike with his friend. Otherwise, as has become clear enough, climbing serves as a means of earning money.

I wonder whether this will be the case in future. This takes me back to Deepak Thapa's statement that in Nepal the new generation of climbers is raising their educational standards.

Contrary to this, in Shimshal, the attainment of education takes people away from climbing. The general perception is that an educated person has a choice; he need not toil as a climber or high-altitude porter.

As described in the first chapter, to attain excellent education is a priority in Shimshal. More and more young people are being sent to colleges and universities by their parents. Their number has increased to the hundreds by now.

Education and first-rate job qualification, and not climbing, is what the future is all about.

Regrettably, the reverse is also true. Students of Qudrat's mountaineering school lack education especially in English. They are hardly familiar with the very basics of the language, with the exception of one or two. Despite their technical skills, as long as this is the case, they will have limited job prospects. They will also lag behind in the competition with their Nepali counterparts.

The question here to ask is whether it would be a deplorable thing if in future, fewer and fewer Shimshalis offered themselves as HAPs on K-2, Nanga Parbat, and other peaks. I think not. It would mean that 'my' high-altitude porters will have achieved their goal: sparing their children from their own hard work by giving them a good education.

Another aspect worth mentioning here relates to the prestige and recognition that can originate from climbing. The HAPs are well aware that Western publishers churn out hundreds of books in which individual climbing celebrities portray themselves, or in which Joe Bloggs profitably describes his adventures in the midst of looming seracs. Others manage to attract massive crowds with their huge slideshows in big auditoriums, and the sponsors queue up at their front doors. At least the Shimshalis believe this to be true.

Unfortunately, in Pakistan, the media attention and public awareness with regards to mountaineering and high-altitude climbers is next to zero if we look beyond the grand old names of Nazir Sabir,[9] Ashraf Aman,[10] and Rajab Shah. Fame and honour have never been a reward for the climbers.

What remains, therefore, is viewing the job pragmatically and without illusions. This level-headedness may be one of the reasons why so many of my interviewees did not extol their deeds: '2002 Gasherbrum-II, German expedition, camp 3, bad weather, finish, end of story'.

It will surprise us to hear that many a high porter, once having arrived at camp 3 or camp 4, forgoes the summit bid. There have been cases in which the expedition leader stopped them. Occasionally, however, it is at their own discretion that they abstain from going any further towards the peak. What is then the slavery for? It affords neither acclaim nor profit but, instead, the ever present risk of being killed in the 'death zone'.

Let me venture a prediction: as long as there is no support from the government, media, and tour operators, climbing will play a marginal role in Shimshal. There are more important, less hazardous, things to do and with more promise for the future.

Notes

1. In the Hunza Valley.
2. HAP: high-altitude porter.
3. ATP: Adventure Tours Pakistan.
4. Kammerlander 2012: 319.
5. Thapa 2008.
6. Thapa 2008: 210.
7. Thapa 2008: 212.
8. In 2012, a Pakistani TV-film maker, Sherbano Saiyid, joined them and made a documentary of two expeditions. She told me that she was planning on further activities with the girls, including 7,000- and 8,000-metre peaks.
9. First Pakistani to summit Mount Everest.
10. First Pakistani to summit K-2, and founder of ATP (Adventure Tours Pakistan).

1.4

The Pakistani Eight-thousand-metre Peaks

MUCH HAS BEEN WRITTEN ABOUT THE FOURTEEN EIGHT-thousand-metre peaks, in general, and the five Pakistani ones, in particular, so I take the freedom to keep it short in this book. Those who are interested in further details and the climbing history of each eight-thousand-metre peak are advised to turn to Hans Kammerlander's *Zurück nach morgen*.

1. Gasherbrum 2 (also called G-II)

- Altitude: 8,035 metres.
- First climbed in 1956 by Austrians Josef Larch, Fritz Moravec, and Hans Willenpart.

G-2 is the second lowest of the fourteen eight-thousand-metre peaks. It has become a much frequented destination for commercially organized expeditions which hire a substantial number of high-altitude porters.

2. Broad Peak

- Altitude: 8,047 metres.

- First climbed in 1957 by Austrians Hermann Buhl, Kurt Diemberger, Markus Schmuck, and Fritz Wintersteller. Broad Peak is thought to be an easy eight-thousand-metre peak but it is often exposed to capricious weather conditions. It is also besieged every year by numerous commercial expeditions.

3. Gasherbrum-I (also called G-I and Hidden Peak)

- Altitude: 8,068 metres.
- First climbed in 1958 by Americans Andy Kauffman and Pete Schoening.

Although G-I ranks among the 'low' eight-thousand-metre peaks, it is technically more demanding than its brother G-II. The name Gasherbrum is derived from the Balti language and means 'Shining Wall'. There are a further four Gasherbrums, none of which reaches eight-thousand metres.

4. Nanga Parbat

- Altitude: 8,125 metres.
- First climbed in 1953 by Austrian Hermann Buhl.

Nanga Parbat has been given, among other terms, the questionable title of 'Killer Mountain'. This is mainly due to the considerable number of deadly accidents which occurred on German expeditions during the 1930s. Incessant rockfalls and constantly tumbling avalanches make the 'Naked Mountain' one of the difficult eight-thousand-metre peaks. Also, for decades it was in the focus of the media, following the tragedy of the two Messner brothers. Günther Messner, Reinhold Messner's younger brother, disappeared on Nanga Parbat in 1970. The circumstances of his death remained obscure for many years and this triggered a venomous fight between Messner and the other expedition members which ended in total estrangement.

5. K-2 (also called Chogori and Mount Godwin-Austen)

- Altitude: 8,611 metres.
- First climbed in 1954 by Italians Lino Lacedelli and Achille Compagnoni.

The 'King of Mountains', as people like to call it, gets everyone to wax lyrical about its beauty. After Mount Everest (8,848 m), it is the second highest mountain on earth but climbing it is by far more difficult. Indeed, K-2 is quite correctly considered the most difficult eight-thousand-metre peak of all. Its symmetric, pyramidal shape is unique. Hundreds of trekkers annually make the pilgrimage along the 60-km Baltoro Glacier to the famed Concordia Place and live their dream of seeing K-2 in all its glory with their own eyes. However, a shockingly large number of people have died on K-2, if you consider how few have reached its summit.

1.5

Three Categories and One of His Own

The Soldiers

IN SHIMSHAL, THE PAKISTAN ARMY IS HELD IN HIGH ESTEEM, even veneration. This is certainly not due to the Shimshalis' patriotism. Their Ismaili identity is more important to them than the Pakistani one, and they are not exactly infatuated with the government in Islamabad. Nor is it any martial spirit in the villagers' character; unconditional love of peace is one of the Aga Khan's basic principles. It may be their passion for all things connected with uniforms, soldierly mannerism, and decoration which has been adopted by Ismaili communities. The volunteers and boy scouts proudly display their uniforms and polished medals at religious festivals.

By far the most significant reasons for the army's popularity are the numerous occasions on which it was of assistance when there was a crisis or the Shimshalis asked for help. I will come to that later.

In the year 1958, the army established its headquarters in Shimshal. It was the onset of the Cold War. In an effort to deter the Americans on the far side of the globe, the Chinese had started to secure their border. This border was in the middle of nowhere, in the wild, deserted, and almost inaccessible Pamirs. All of a sudden, Chinese soldiers on horses had advanced and reached the Baraldu River. They had bravely vanquished passes and precipitous ridges, and were now determined to stay put. In the no-man's land, among wolves and snow leopards, they erected stone barracks and built a stretch of halfway negotiable road which can still be seen today.

These unpleasant activities, of course, called for the arrival of the Pakistan Army to this region. Initially, it was fifty soldiers who were stationed in Shimshal. They fought with the Chinese who had hauled heavy artillery over vast distances of the jagged terrain.

Today, proximity to the Chinese border is not a problem for Shimshal—of course, if you don't count the phantom of 'restricted area' which turns up every now and then. Whenever it materializes, it means that foreigners cannot go beyond the police post at the entrance of the Shimshal Valley. This, in turn, triggers general confusion and annoyance until the affair turns out to be a rumour or an arbitrary step of a corrupt official. Otherwise, Shimshalis affirm their friendship with the Chinese (which, of course, they should as they also received relief supplies from China during the Attabad disaster).

As stated above, there have been several operations which granted the army the status of a benefactor in Shimshal. Two memorable events in this regard should be quoted here.

In 1997, an army general flew a helicopter to Shimshal carrying the first tractor plus threshing machine to the village. This was truly a trail-blazing event.

In the winter of 2008–9, a huge snowfall stopped supplies from being carried to the yak shepherds beyond the Shimshal Pass. On the satellite phone, the villagers called the army for help which instantly sent a helicopter that dropped provisions for the shepherds in the Baraldu Valley.

The army is an uncannily powerful entity in Pakistan. It does not only run the military but also huge portions of real estate business and all kinds of manufacturing and service industries. Time and again, the country's political reign has also been in the hands of military dictators.

For Shimshalis, the army is also a welcome employer. Where else in Pakistan do you get a secure salary, or hope for early retirement (possible after 25 years of service), or receive your old-age pension on an enviably regular basis?

Presently, about forty Shimshalis serve as soldiers in conflict areas such as the infamous Siachen Glacier in Kashmir or in Waziristan on the Afghan border, or on a UN Blue-Helmet mission in Africa.

There are two retired soldiers among 'my' climbers.

2. The High-altitude Porters (HAPs)

The HAPs are my true heroes. It is for them that I have written this book.

Whoever has hauled a backpack of 12 or more kilograms to the summit of a European mountain can guess what it means to carry 15, 16, or even 17 kilograms on the way from base camp (at 5,000 metres) to camp 1 and simultaneously manoeuvre through glacier icefalls. On the ascent to the higher camps, the load may diminish but similarly does the atmospheric pressure, which at 8,000 metres, is only a third of what we are used to in the lowlands. High-altitude sickness which can commence at 3,000 metres, does not exempt high porters from its symptoms: raging headaches, palpitations, loss of appetite, sleeplessness, and sleep apnoea, and at the worst, pulmonary or cerebral oedema.

Moreover, as can be learned from Göran Kropp (and many confirm it from personal experience as well), reasoning ability declines to a shocking extent at high altitude. In his book *Ultimate High: My Everest Odyssey*[1], the Swede writes that a person of average intelligence, at an elevation of 8,000 metres, comprehends the meaning of a sentence only half as well as a six-year-old child at sea level. In such circumstances, high-altitude porters often have to carry, besides the regular loads, the supplementary oxygen bottles which are supposed to mitigate symptoms of high-altitude sickness in the clients and help them to reach the summit.

I would like to emphasize, however, that there are also Western climbers who as a matter of principle refuse to rely on both HAP service and the support of supplementary oxygen, and I do not only refer to the likes of Kammerlander or Kaltenbrunner.[2]

3. The Aces

The aces can also be called 'star climbers' or 'self-made men'. Two friends, Qudrat Ali and Shaheen Baig, fall under this category from Shimshal.

Early enough they knew how to make their fledgling enterprises[3] public on colourful picture postcards. But it was not without some initial years of high-portering that they succeeded in establishing their own company, Shams Alpine, in 2005. With this move, they entered an uncertain terrain since there are dozens of competing tour operators.

Shams Alpine has not proved to be a very profitable business.

With regards to climbing standards, Qudrat and Shaheen

openly declare that they feel superior to their elders (the friends were both born in 1969). They like to emphasize the difference that lies between the mere strength applied by the former, and their own technical climbing, i.e. climbing with super lightweight, power-saving aluminium, and titanium tools.

Both have prospered elsewhere from their mountaineering skills. Shaheen smiles and, in a disarmingly suave manner, speaks of 'good money, big money, lots of money'. The friends capitalize on their skills in the service of a big oil company which hires climbers for the so-called field work. They have been in Yemen, Iraq, and Pakistan as senior employees who answer for the safety of their colleagues. It is for this reason that they are rarely present in Shimshal. In September 2012, when I tried to get hold of Shaheen for an interview, he excused himself and slipped away.

That is why, regrettably, my eulogy on Shaheen and his achievements has to be condensed into a single compelling sentence: he is one of Shimshal's greatest climbers.

For the sake of justice, I am doing the same with his friend Qudrat Ali. His climbing biography has been recorded in my book about his wife Lal Paree, *When Allah Says No* (*Wenn Allah nein sagt*, Verlag Neue Literatur, 2010). It is based on a two-hour interview which is still valid and accurate.

4. The Exception

Ali Musa does not fit in any of the three categories, the reason of which will be clarified in his own chapter. Incidentally, he has compiled a file on the Shimshali climbers' achievements, which unfortunately ends on the year 2001 and does not always tally with what the climbers told me.

Notes

1. Kropp 1998.
2. The Austrian Gerlinde Kaltenbrunner is the first woman to have scaled all fourteen eight-thousand-metre peaks without supplementary oxygen.
3. For example the 'first ski climb' starting from Shimshal which they conducted in the 1990s.

Section Two

The Life Sketches

The following life sketches of Shimshal's climbers and HAPs are arranged along the sequence of my interviews with them. This random sequencing works best for me since any other arrangement might exude the impression of my own preferences—something that I would never attempt.

1. Two winter shepherds in traditional clothing (1992).

2. First training of climbers at Malangutti Glacier in 1995 with Rajab Shah (tallest person in red jacket).

3. Mohammad Ullah.

4. Official expedition greeting card; seventh from left:
Mohammad Ullah, eighth: Yousaf Khan.

5. Qurban Mohammad.

6. One of Qurban Mohammad's numerous certificates.

7. Sarwar Ali.

To whom it may concern,

This is to certify that Mr. Sarwar Ali, s/o Mirza Ali, climbed the summit of Broad Peak on July 20th, 2013, to help search and rescue 3 Iranian members who lost their way descending the summit of Broad Peak upon climbing a new route on west face.

I'm fully satisfied and gratefull for his help.

Regards,

Ramin Shojaei
Iranian Expedition Leader
July 22, 2013

8. Letter of Recommendation from the Iranian expedition leader thanking Sarwar Ali for his self-sacrificing commitment on the summit of Broad Peak (2013).

9. Meherban Shah.

10. Meherban's son Ghulam Ali Shah, who was killed by an avalanche
on Sonia Peak in 2001.

11. Calendar photo of 1995: Rajab Shah and Meherban Shah on K-2.

12. Calendar photo of 1995: the infamous Bottleneck below the K-2 summit.

13. Farhad Khan.

14. Hasil Shah in front of his tourist lodge.

15. Hasil's business card (front).

CURRICULUM VITAE

1. Climbed Sonia Peak (6,150m) in 2005.
2. Climbed Muztagnata (7,547m) in 2004.
3. First Summitler of Sun Rise/Year Gatak Peak (6,354m) in 2002.
4. Climbed K-2 (8,611m) in 1999.
5. Climbed Gasharburum-II (8,035m) in 2003, 1998 & 1996.
6. Climbed Spantik Golden Peak (7,027m) in 1996 & 2005.
7. Climbed Passu Peak (7,284m) in 1996.
8. Climbed Quz Sar Peak (6,050m) in 1992.
9. Climbed Minglig Sar (6,200m) in 1991, 1996, 2000, 2001 & 2004.
10. Peer Peak (6,075m) in 2009

16. Hasil's business card (back).

17. Hasil's aspiration to climb K-2 as depicted in his sister's tapestry.

18. Hasil on the summit of G-II (1997).

19. Amruddin.

20. Amruddin with his daughter, Bano.

21. Amruddin on the summit of Nanga Parbat (2001).

22. Amruddin on the House's Chimney below Camp 2, K-2 (2004).

23. Aziz Baig.

24. A tangle of ropes fixed in the Diamir Wall of Nanga Parbat (1997).

25. Aziz Baig on the summit of Nanga Parbat
with three Tibetans (1997).

26. Aziz Baig on K-2, above Camp 2 (2005).

27. Aziz Baig near Camp 4 on K-2 (2005).

28. Amin Ullah Baig.

29. Rajab Shah.

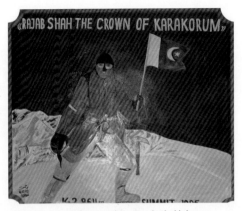

30. One of the murals in Rajab Shah's house.

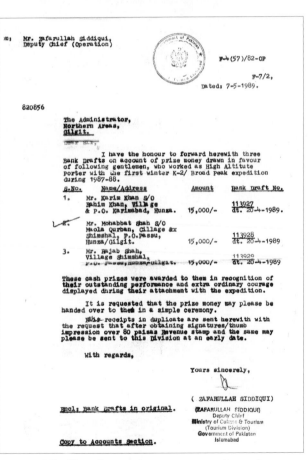

TO: Mr. Zafarullah Siddiqui,
Deputy Chief (Operation)

F-4(57)/82-OP

F-7/2,
Dated: 7-5-1989.

820856

The Administrator,
Northern Areas,
Gilgit.

        I have the honour to forward herewith three
Bank Drafts on account of prize money drawn in favour
of following gentlemen, who worked as High Altitude
Porter with the first winter K-2/ Broad Peak expedition
during 1987-88.

S.No.	Name/Address	Amount	Bank Draft No.
1.	Mr. Karim Khan s/o Rahim Khan, Village & P.O. Karimabad, Hunza.	15,000/-	113927 dt. 20-4-1989.
2.	Mr. Mohabbat Shah s/o Maola Qurban, Cillage &x Shimshal, P.O.Passu, Hunza/Gilgit.	15,000/-	113928 dt. 20-4-1989
3.	Mr. Rajab Shah, Village Shimshal, P.O. Passu,Hunza/Gilgit.	15,000/-	113929 dt. 20-4-1989

        These cash prizes were awarded to them in recognition of
their outstanding performance and extra ordinary courage
displayed during their attachment with the expedition.

        It is requested that the prize money may please be
handed over to them in a simple ceremony.

        The receipts in duplicate are sent herewith with
the request that after obtaining signatures/thumb
impression over 80 paisas Revenue stamp and the same may
please be sent to this Division at an early date.

        With regards,

Yours sincerely,

(ZAFARULLAH SIDDIQUI)

(ZAFARULLAH SIDDIQUI)
Deputy Chief
Ministry of Culture & Tourism
(Tourism Division)
Government of Pakistan
Islamabad

Encl: Bank Drafts in original.

Copy to Accounts Section.

31. Official letter documenting extra payments given to three
high-altitude porters.

32. Rajab Shah (place and time unknown).

33. Rajab Shah as climbing instructor (place and time unknown).

34. The two friends, Meherban Shah and Rajab Shah.

35. Syed Ahmed.

36. Syed Ahmed on the summit of Spantik (1999).

37. Ezat Ullah Baig.

38. Mounds of snow at Camp 1 on G-II (2003).

39. Ezat Ullah Baig above Camp 2 on G-II (2004).

40. Sabz Ali.

41. Meherban Karim (right) and Amin Ullah Baig at the Gilkey
Memorial, K-2.

42. Meherban Karim on
the summit of G-I (2004).

43. Meherban Karim's widow Haji Parveen
with daughter, Umbreen.

44. Yousaf Khan.

45. Yousaf Khan on Broad Peak between Camp 1 and 2 (1994).

46. Yousaf Khan and Mohammad Ullah at Camp 3 on Nanga Parbat (1997).

47. Ali Musa.

48. Jehan Baig at K-2 base camp (date unknown).

49. One of the last photos of Meherban Karim and Jehan Baig at K-2 base camp. Third from right in front row is Jehan Baig; seventh is Meherban Karim. Second from left in third row is Hugues d' Aubarède, the French climber.

50. Jehan Baig, Meherban Shah, and Aziz Qurban, probably on G-II (date unknown).

51. Qudrat Ali, Amin Ullah Baig, and Jehan Baig on the summit of G-II(date unknown).

52. Jehan Baig digs up a tent at a high-elevation camp (place and time unknown).

53. Jehan Baig's widow Gul Dana and his mother Naseeb Begum.

54. Farzar Khan.

55. Farzar Khan at K-2 (date unknown).

56. Farzar Khan and Ezat Ullah Baig on the summit of G-II (2001).

57. Tafat Shah.

58. Group photo of a striking number of Shimshalis at K-2, probably in 2005. First from left in second row is Shaheen Baig; third is Amruddin; fifth is Meherban Karim; sixth is Ezat Ullah Baig. First from left in front row is Meherban Shah; second is Farzar Khan; fifth is Aziz Baig.

59. Pakistani soldiers in camouflage fatigues on the Siachen Glacier at the Pak-India border.

2.1

Mohammad Ullah

Retired soldier, born 1954

MOHAMMAD ULLAH HAS A SHORT, SLIGHT BUILD, AND A FACE
furrowed by a hundred smiles. When we (myself and my
interpreter Samad Karim) arrive at his home, he hails us in
working gear, i.e. baseball cap and work pants, for it is harvesting
time and every hand is being called for almost around the clock.
The fact that he allots us time—when others will postpone
talking or even refuse their consent for the interview—reveals
that this is important to him. When I reach for my camera, he
excuses himself for a moment; he wishes to dress formally for the
photos. Clad in a freshly pressed shirt, the traditional woollen
cap, and a pair of dignified trousers, he reappears. He has also
brought his awards: metal sheets, engraved, polished, and boxed
in faded velvet, which he wants to be seen in the picture.

For the interview, we avoid the family bustle and settle down
in a nearby room that seems to be newly built. Mohammad
Ullah apologizes for its bleakness and inhospitable atmosphere
but the place's peace is more important for our purpose than
comfort or beauty.

He is sitting cross-legged while he talks and rocking his
upper body which, just like his easy and relaxed gait, suggests
somebody younger than his 59 years.

He smiles a lot with his small eyes and affords a lot of patience while explaining complicated things, for example the old game *Tuk Sur* played by children. I do not comprehend anything at first. He jumps to his feet and heads outside. From the firewood, he fetches both a reasonably straight branch and a small knot which he puts on the floor. He then raises the branch and hits the knot which scoots around unpredictably. While the knot is still in the air, he hits it again, dead on target. This is the way of Tuk Sur: only the second hit is to be performed by a second player. Nowadays, the boys passionately play cricket instead.

Mohammad Ullah lives in a large, traditional family. During his childhood twenty people packed the house. He is the youngest of four brothers and two sisters.

He attended school until third grade which cost him five years. This was because he played truant during exam week and therefore could not proceed further in classes.

His teacher was Ghulam Sultan from Gulmit. In 1966, Daulat Amin, the 'father of education' in Shimshal took over.[1] Every morning there was a prayer before lessons. It was one and the same class for all students regardless of their ages. Rajab Shah, for instance, was among them a 'senior', as were Mohammad's peers Yousaf Khan and Nehal Baig. Similarly, there was one Urdu textbook only because no other subject was being taught.[2] The pupils also had to share this lone book which meant that they had to behave virtuously. And they did because they had huge respect for the teacher. As long as he was standing in front of them, the boys were innocence personified. Hardly had they made their escape from the classroom when they began to fight and wrestle. 'Just as boys are,' Mohammad laughs.

During classes, football and volleyball were played, and

also the local games *Tuk Sur* and *Pisht Mao*. The latter goes as follows: two equally sized groups of two to five members each are pitched against one another. While one group waits as long as agreed upon, just like in hide-and-seek, the other one rushes out in all directions. Each player, preferably in hidden places, scrapes together little heaps of sand and memorizes his location. The first group then goes searching for them. Those who find a heap will level it. The higher the numbers of undiscovered heaps, the more points for group number two.

Mohammad Ullah tells me that his two best friends, Ismail Khan and Ali Shafa, have already passed away. His mother died when he was ten or eleven years old. His elder sisters substituted for her which is a common thing in Shimshal.

Every summer in his early childhood he went on the three-day trek to Shuwerth, one of the high-pasture settlements, and stayed there for four weeks with the women who look after the yaks, goats, and sheep.

When I question him whether visitors or even foreigners showed up in Shimshal at that time, he shakes his head: neither researchers nor merchants or government officials of any sort, let alone tourists.[3]

Self-sufficient as they were, the Shimshalis during that era exclusively wore things that they had made with their own hands. These included woven coats, knitted gloves, or boots made of goat's skin, with the furry side in. This lasted until the 1990s (cf. photo).

Little did I learn about the medical drugs and 'therapies' prevalent in the past. Headaches seem to have been treated with old, smelly butter which was rubbed into the scalp. Diarrhoea was cured with *tsmik*, which is cheese diluted in hot water—a treatment still in use today. Those who suffered from a pain in the back wrapped hot embers in cloth and applied the pack to the sore spot.

As early as in Mohammad Ullah's childhood years, the first vaccination campaign for children reached Shimshal. Although he does not recall the name of the illness that was meant to be prevented, he does remember the procedure: the upper arm was scratched open with a sharp blade, and the serum was rubbed into the cut by a team of doctors who came from Hunza once in a year.

From all my interviewees I wanted to know when they first left their village for bigger cities, and what their destination and mission was. It was in 1970 when Mohammad first took this trip. Back then, he was sixteen years of age. He walked the 65 kilometres to Passu in order to spend four weeks with his sister who had married there.

In 1972, Mohammad Ullah joined the Pakistan Army. It was another seventeen years before he reached one of the truly big goals: the summit of Nanga Parbat.

Climbing was merely one part of his military training conducted in Abbottabad, a city around 100 km north-west of Islamabad. Abbottabad has been a military centre since the time of British colonial rule. Far away from Nanga Parbat and the Karakorums, the mountains around Abbottabad are neither high nor glaciated and snow-covered. Still, they make a suitable training ground for technical practise. It was there that the soldiers learned how to tie and fix ropes and prusik knots, clip karabiners, and apply ascenders and rappelling devices. Not to mention the safety rules, rescue measures, and meteorology.

In 1989, Mohammad Ullah and Rajab Shah from Shimshal were the first Pakistanis to reach the summit of Nanga Parbat. This deserves to be emphasized because the names of Rajab Shah and Mohammad Ullah are not even remotely as prominent as those of Nazir Sabir and Ashraf Aman, the first Pakistanis to summit Mount Everest and K-2 respectively.

Mohammad remembers details of this army expedition. There were seventeen members, with their leader being the very notable Colonel Sher Khan. Three Shimshalis, the two soldiers Mohammad Ullah and Yousaf Khan, and Rajab Shah were in this expedition. Rajab Shah participated as the spokesman and representative of the HAPs. The equipment, according to Mohammad, was exquisite. All the goods were branded and imported from Germany, Italy, and France. Everything else pertaining to logistics and management was in Pakistani hands. The army had bought life insurance for its members.

Early on in the expedition, on day two or three after arriving at the base camp, Mohammad had to witness and come to terms with a shocking incident. On a dangerous rock face between camp 1 and camp 2, a Korean expedition member climbed with an old rope, which tore. He fell to his death. Mohammad helped to retrieve his body. The deceased was sheathed in his sleeping bag, tied to a stretcher, and carried to the base camp. A helicopter picked his body from there and took it to Rawalpindi. Owing to this fatality, the Koreans cancelled their expedition.

Initially, the army expedition went according to schedule. The site of camp 3 had been selected and the tents had been pitched. The members were eager to make the summit bid but the weather changed. Gale-force winds blew, and hail and snowfall started, leaving them with no choice but to descend to the base camp as fast as possible. To their surprise, in no way were the circumstances any better at the base camp site either. The base camp was also snowed in. Twelve days at stretch, they were not able to venture out beyond the camp. Mohammad recalls this with a smile and tells me that the situation was not absolutely grim because they got better food. Fresh bread, for instance, was made there on a daily basis as was the case with rice, meat, and vegetables. In the high camps where human appetite dwindles anyway, climbers have to make do with soup and tea, stale biscuits, and hard-frozen chocolate. Sometimes only the dried apricots, which the Shimshalis bring along from home, keep them going up there. Occasionally, these apricots become backup supply when the food in a high camp simply runs out.

When the window of good weather opened after a long standstill, the team did their best to exploit it. Not only did they reach camp 3 within three days, but they also erected a fourth camp above an avalanche-infested area thinking that it should enable them to climb to the summit on the fourth day.

Bad weather struck again on the day the summit climb was planned. A storm had set in during the previous night which was about to rip apart the fabric of the tent tarpaulins. After a long period of indecision and a futile wait for better weather, four members left the camp. These were Colonel Sher Khan, Flight Lieutenant Mohammad Atta, Rajab Shah, and Mohammad Ullah. Yousaf Khan did not feel it quite right to go any further in such adverse conditions. Also among the climbers was a German whose name none of the three Shimshalis can recall. He had joined the Pakistanis from camp 2 and shared a rope with them.

Mohammad says that due to unfavourable weather, the departure had been as late as 10 o'clock. What followed was sheer battle with the cold, blizzard, bottomless snow, a lack of oxygen (none of them used bottled oxygen), flagging muscles, misgivings, and fear.

After more than nine hours—which they endured with enormous willpower—they stood on the peak of Nanga Parbat but not in good shape. They had to cling to each other in order to prevent the raging winds from sweeping them into the void. They began to descend instantly. Wasn't it against all rules and wisdom to arrive on an eight-thousander summit at this late hour, and in such weather?

With the last bit of their strength and a totally blurred vision, they found camp 4 at around 2 o'clock in the morning. Soon they became aware that one of them was missing. Mohammad Atta had not arrived with the rest!

None of them could gather the energy to go out again and start a search. Each had been stretched to his human limits and focused on his own survival in the hostile circumstances.

After the death of the Korean, which he had witnessed from close up, this was already the second terrible experience for the eigh-thousander newcomer, Mohammad Ullah: to be reduced to a shivering, exhausted creature, to crawl into a clammy sleeping bag, and simultaneously to know, one of us is still out there in the blizzard. Where is he? Is he alive? Is he dying? Is he already dead? How will we find him?

Fortunately, Mohammad Atta was found at daybreak. He was alive and was taken down to the base camp. However, with his severe frostbite, he had to be flown out immediately by helicopter.

For Mohammad Ullah and Rajab Shah, this was not only the first eight-thousand-metre summit but they were also the first Pakistanis to stand on top of Nanga Parbat. What a feat!

The news was spread by radio in Gojal.[4] Mohammad's family prepared an ample reception for him. A sheep was slaughtered and the ceremonial bread *ptuk* was made. Later, all villagers were invited to another festive meal with meat and chapatis.

Unfortunately, Mohammad's next eight-thousand-metre peak success has faded in his memory. He cannot even recall the precise year of his victorious climb to Gasherbrum-I. It must have been in 1990, in a joint expedition of the Pakistani and French armies. For him, what is far more significant is the fact that he climbed the infamous Nanga Parbat once again in 1997.

This was also a joint expedition—this time of the Pakistani and Chinese Alpine Clubs. In the end, two Pakistanis and six Tibetans arrived on top of Nanga Parbat.

Mohammad openly admits that on this tour he narrowly escaped death—thanks to the alertness and sacrifice of another Shimshali, Aziz Baig. It is intriguing to compare how one and the same event is recorded by two different characters. Aziz Baig's story is noted in his own chapter.

Mohammad says he reached the summit in total exhaustion, so much so that he flung himself down on the snow and wanted to lie there forever. He did not inform others of his alarming condition. He gritted his teeth and forced himself to stand. He tried the first tentative step but collapsed. He gave it another try but collapsed as he had become miserably weak. It seemed to be the end. His fellow Shimshali, Aziz Baig, had already started to descend but in the middle of it he stopped and looked back. He stood where he was, shouted at the top of his lungs, and told Mohammad to gather his strength. It took Mohammad a lot of time and willpower to take a single step and get moving again. Aziz kept supporting and steadying him; he had to pull and push him continuously. When the tents came within sight, Mohammad asked his friend to hurry ahead and make some soup for him as he needed it to restore his energy. He did feel a bit better afterwards but realized that the problem had not actually been solved. The 'problem' is not something Mohammad expands on, except that he did two things: he rubbed oil on his forehead and took a tablet that he considered suitable.

He does not disclose how he survived the following night; he might have lost consciousness, off and on.

Shortly after this crisis, Mohammad was so bright-eyed and full of life that he instantly set off on the long trek to the high pastures in Voulio in order to participate in the annual yak race and to climb the six-thousand-metre peak, Mingli Sar, with a handful of teenage boys. Upon his return, a sheep was again slaughtered in his honour.

Mingli Sar (6,015 metres), the classic in the Shimshal Pamir, has been climbed an uncountable number of times by all 'my' climbers including Mohammad Ullah. Mingli is generally noted under 'also-ran' and not regarded as a special accomplishment. In his file, Ali Musa has listed some other six- and seven-thousand-metre peaks under Mohammad's name but he does not mention Mingli Sar.

In the year 1993, i.e. after less than 25 years of service, Mohammad retired from the Pakistan Army as a havildar.[5] He had been fortunate to evade any serious combat operations during his army affiliation. Amongst other places, he had been stationed on the legendary and infamous Siachen Glacier in Pakistan's disputed border area with India. Rumour has it that it is the freezing temperatures and high-altitude sickness[6] that kills the soldiers on Siachen rather than fighting against the 'enemy'. However, Mohammad points out that he did not have a bad life up there—thanks to the first-class equipment. During that period, two to three men lived in one insulated tent; today it is igloos with triple insulation layers that house five to seven soldiers.

There was a two-month vacation but when stationed in remote regions such as Siachen, the soldiers sometimes had to serve for twelve months straight before they got leaves of absence.

At his leave-taking, Mohammad Ullah received two awards: the *Tamgha-e-Basalat* or *TBT* and the *Tamgha-e-Khidmat* or *TK3*. Apart from the honour, these medals manifest themselves in material form too. Luckily, with the *TBT,* Mohammad got a piece of land in Gilgit. He says it was worth 30,000 rupees and would be ten times more than that today—the equivalent of around 3,000 euros. He sold that piece of land. From the *TK3*, Mohammad continues to receive a monthly payment of seventy-five rupees. Moreover, he gets his retirement pension which amounts to 8,000 rupees per month.

To this day, Mohammad Ullah is healthy and in good shape. As member of the Ismaili Volunteers, he also contributes to community welfare. His children are comparatively young because there had been no offspring from his first marriage. His first wife died in 1983 after nine years of marriage. Two years later, he remarried but it was not until 2000 that his first daughter was born. Today he has two daughters and a son.

When he sees us off, Mohammad expresses his appreciation for the interview in a wholehearted and almost exuberant manner. He adds that the younger generation is virtually ignorant of the climbers' achievements, which Samad confirms. Mohammad says that he will feel gratified when this book comes out and highlights what has been undisclosed and unmentioned for so many years.

Notes

1. When I interviewed Daulat Amin in 2008 about the history of education in Shimshal, he kept quiet about his predecessor Ghulam Sultan.
2. However, cf. a different version under Yousaf Khan.
3. John Mock writes in his *Lonely Planet*: 'Shimshal was closed to outsiders until 1986.'
4. Gojal is a region in Gilgit-Baltistan where Shimshal is located.
5. Urdu word for 'constable'.
6. It is believed that humans cannot survive for long at elevations of more than ca. 4,700 metres.

2.2

Qurban Mohammad

High-altitude porter and rescuer, born 1955

I HAVE KNOWN QURBAN SINCE 2002, WHEN HE ESCORTED
me on my solo trekking tour across Chafchingol Pass. He
was an extremely considerate and energetic companion,
constantly smiling, always modest, and unacquainted with
the English language.

His English has improved to some degree in the past years
and his self-confidence has clearly increased. Upon our
arrival, the first thing he does is hand me a newspaper article
from DAWN[1] of September 2009, which portrays him as a
mountain rescuer, and carries a photo of him 'in action'. Now
that is a good reason to feel proud of oneself.

Even though it turns out that the article contained a
number of errors, one thing is undeniably true. 'Weather-
beaten poker face' is what describes Qurban's physiognomy
best. He makes this face, for example, when he smiles
roguishly at my inquiry about his year of birth because he
just does not know it.[2] When I ask about the duration of
his schooling, he doubtfully responds that it could be one
year maximum. The date of his wedding is something that he
clearly doesn't remember.

The increase in his self-confidence is also due to his son's efforts to promote him on the Internet. It is to Muqeem that he submitted all his photos and documents. He tells me that I will have to approach Muqeem if I need anything of that kind. Qurban Mohammad turned to mountaineering relatively late. In the mid-1990s he joined a training session on Malangutti Glacier which was conducted by Rajab Shah. On his first 8,000-metre summit in 1998, he was the novice beside the seasoned climbers Rajab Shah, Meherban Shah, and Aziz Baig. For eleven more years he worked as a high-altitude porter and mountain rescuer.

The year 2009 brought him a serious health crisis. Consequently, he had to discontinue high-altitude portering for the time being. I am not sure whether Qurban will want to resume slaving on the Pakistani eight-thousand-metre peaks.

His memory fails occasionally during the interview. Years and dates are not perfectly accurate. It is from his son that I learn, for example, that he went to K-2 thrice, and not only on the one fatal occasion in 2009.

Muqeem's attitude towards his father's climbing is ambivalent. On the one hand, he asserts that it is a deplorable thing for fathers to risk their lives in an effort to finance their children's education, as was the case with Qurban. On the other hand, although Muqeem closely witnessed the ruinous effects that the drudgery on K-2 had had on his father's health, he laconically says, 'He is in love with adventure sport.' He does not wish to stop his father from climbing. If he feels fine then why not.

Qurban's first eight-thousand-metre expedition took him to Gasherbrum-II. It was a Japanese team of fourteen members that had hired quite a number of HAPs from both Shimshal and Baltistan. Figures and names vary among my interviewees because another Japanese expedition, with a crew of the national TV channel NHK, was on the mountain. The chapters on Hazil Shah and Ali Musa will deal with that.

As mentioned, Qurban was a beginner among the high-altitude porters. He smiles when he tells me that he intended to show off his strength and hauled overly heavy loads initially. This cost him precious energy but instead of discarding his excessive zeal, he continued to 'prove his capability' as a rescuer and saviour in extreme situations.

Having arrived at camp 4 at 7,400 metres, the Japanese discovered something unbelievable: one of the gas burners was missing! Someone had forgotten to take it along from camp 3. Dispensing with it was totally out of the question. It meant that they would not be able to make enough tea for everybody, both in the evening and a few hours later, for the summit bid. Therefore, one of them had to descend as much as 500 metres of altitude to camp 3, and that too very quickly. Qurban was the most appropriate HAP for this task. The fact that he had sufficient spare energy for this exploit is remarkable in itself. Moreover, he proved his toughness by joining the others shortly afterwards on the summit bid.

It is at the tour leader's discretion whether or not the HAPs are allowed to make the summit bid. As already stated, they are not always keen on it. However, more often than not, they have to climb or are even forced to join. This is because they are the ones who must break the trail and, implicitly, answer for the safety of the members. Some Western climbers literally have to be held by their hands. In Ali Musa's interview, the readers will learn that an ever-increasing number of expeditions include people whose technical skills are meagre beyond belief. He has witnessed some 'climbers' who cannot even handle crampons or an ascender. When, in the so-called death zone, exhaustion, high-altitude sickness, and declining mental capacity set in, the high-altitude porter becomes a saviour of lives just by providing another bottle of oxygen to the victim. Qurban says that on his 1998 expedition, Rajab Shah, Meherban Shah, Aziz Baig, and he had fixed all the ropes and thus the Japanese leader let them make the summit bid with six members.

Of Qurban's next expeditions, I only learn the bare facts. In the year 2001, he reached the top of Broad Peak; in 2004 a summit bid of Gasherbrum-II failed. Similarly, in 2005, he had to turn back on Nanga Parbat along with Qudrat Ali and Meherban Karim. In 2006 and 2007, he climbed the seven-thousand-metre peak Spantik with Iranians and Spaniards respectively.

Qurban's first rescue mission was sometime in between 2005 and 2007—he does not remember the year accurately. It was on Nanga Parbat. A climber—Qurban only recalls that he was 'a famous man' but not his name or nationality—had been on the summit, and upon his return to camp 4 found that his food supplies had all run out. Due to his illustrious background, this person had taken precautionary measures prior to his expedition. He had arranged a helicopter which was at standby in Skardu and, in case of an emergency, could take a team of rescuers to Nanga Parbat. Unfortunately, this emergency had now materialized. The man called on his satellite phone. Qurban and a couple of Baltis were flown to the Diamir base camp of Nanga Parbat. They started climbing immediately. They were carrying a satellite phone with which they could receive the occasional call from the man waiting up there in thin air. Each time, his voice became feebler, his words more desperate.

They found him dead. It was shortly before their arrival that he must have passed away. Qurban says that the Baltis refused to touch the dead body. It was him who had to take care of everything: put him in his sleeping bag, tie him up, and fix him to a rope using which he could be lifted by a helicopter which never came. They had descended to a lower altitude and waited for the helicopter in vain. Therefore, Qurban salvaged the man's belongings—his watch and a camera—in order to return them to his wife in Skardu, and finally buried the corpse in the snow.

The rescuers had been promised 0.5 million rupees each. However, due to corruption, this amount shrank to 50,000 rupees per person.

At this point, I must note an episode that cannot be dated even after close investigation. It is about two rescue operations that Qurban performed on Broad Peak in close succession. For the first, he was called because a woman had contracted severe frostbite on both hands and feet during the summit bid. Qurban says that he single-handedly carried her alone from camp 4 to camp 2. Upon arrival, it seemed fair to him to rest and have some tea and bread to restore his energy. He had hardly settled down when the radio stirred to life. His services, it said, were required once again. He was to get to his feet and climb rapidly to camp 4 again. A distance of more than 1,000 altitude metres, in a region above 6,000 metres! Qurban dropped the bread, took a sip of tea, and set off. This time it was high-altitude sickness and a few frostbitten toes that one German climber was suffering from, whose name Qurban does not remember. In order to descend, he needed an escort and a pair of strong shoulders. It took them two days to reach base camp. The man was exceptionally tall and heavy which did not ease Qurban's task. On the way down, his condition improved rapidly, and so did his humour. He did not stop chatting, even on hazardous terrains. Qurban hardly believed his ears when he learned that his charge was planning to climb Gasherbrum-II straight after Broad Peak. He completed his recovery in base camp and gave Qurban his binoculars out of gratitude. A few days later, he died in an avalanche on Gasherbrum-II.

I want to know if Qurban, after this double rescue action, finally realized that he had reached his limits. He merely laughs and says the up-and-down movement helped him to 'acclimatize'.

In the summer of 2008—when within two days eleven climbers died on K-2, which included two Sherpas and two Shimshalis—Qurban worked for a Spanish team on Gasherbrum-II. This expedition did not pass without drama either. Qurban had been ordered to stay in camp 3 while the members planned to move to camp 4 and then to the summit. In the small hours of the night, Qurban heard static on the radio and the leader's anxious voice told him to get up instantly and take a full oxygen bottle to camp 4. Big problems had brewed up there! With the help of his headlamp, Qurban tried to identify the bamboo poles with little red rags that marked the route. This must have been a gruelling job to carry out at midnight, to say the least. He arrived at camp 4 and learned the reason of his arduous trek: one of the Spaniards, after being exposed to the fierce winds in the summit region, was frostbitten on both hands, nose, and several other parts of his face. Since his hands were no longer able to grip and clutch, as the use of an ice axe requires, there was only one remedy: he had to be carried down. In cooperation with the Spanish team members, Qurban hauled the injured man from camp 4 to base camp. A helicopter picked him up from there and flew him to Skardu. Qurban also went to Skardu before long. It was not until then that the news of the disaster on K-2 on 1–2 August reached him. Jehan Baig and Meherban Karim of Shimshal had perished in this disastrous incident.

In the year 2009, when Qurban worked on K-2 for the third time (he does not mention his first and second experience), he overstretched his physical resources in a reckless way and paid dearly for it. This is my own point of view. Qurban continues reporting impassively.

An American, whose right foot was half amputated due to frostbite, hired Qurban Mohammad as HAP. The two of them planned to climb the Cesen Route. However, members of another expedition prevented them from using their fixed ropes above camp 1 so they had to return to base camp. Qurban had to go to camp 1 once again to pack up the tent and other equipment, and take it down. While he was ascending, an avalanche hit his route. These words are easily written but I assume Qurban has not revealed to me what terror came over him. I need not expand on the phenomenology and the horror of avalanches because, on the one hand, they have been the subject of innumerable texts; on the other, I do not wish to pre-empt Amin Ullah Baig's unique and gripping report of his avalanche experience. Qurban level-headedly says that the shock wave swept him to the edge of the avalanche where he remained unscathed. At base camp, the American had observed everything and concluded, 'Qurban is gone.' Qurban laughs about that.

Afterwards, Qurban and the American joined a different expedition and tried the Abruzzi Route. What happened then is described in the words of Qurban's son Muqeem, who wrote the story in close detail and sent it to me in an e-mail. Snow masses on K-2 in the summer of 2009 were so extraordinary that, in the end, no climber reached the summit. Qurban escorted the new group to above 8,000 metres. From there they wanted to send him down again but he was of a different opinion. He was convinced that he could make himself useful on the summit bid so he stayed. Deprived of oxygen, he awaited several futile attempts at this extreme altitude in thin air. Muqeem says that his father hardly ate anything and drank just the smallest sips of water.

Later on when Qurban made the demanding trek back to Skardu, he began to feel pain in his stomach. Whenever he tried to eat something, his system could not keep it in and he had to throw up. Upon arrival in Skardu, he called Muqeem who told him to board a bus instantly and come to a hospital in Islamabad. This seemed a bit panicky to Qurban. He thought he could get adequate treatment in Skardu as well. Muqeem was fully aware that Skardu's doctors were probably experts in frostbite but not so much in stomach problems such as his father's. Yet he failed to persuade Qurban. On the contrary, since his condition had improved a little, he travelled to Hunza and informed Muqeem that first and foremost he wanted to have a family reunion in Shimshal. Muqeem tore his hair out over his father's obstinacy. Very quickly, his condition deteriorated once again, so much so that Lal Paree, the health official, finally persuaded him to go to Islamabad.

On the evening of his arrival, before the next day's appointment at the hospital, Muqeem invited some cousins for dinner in honour of his father. While standing at the kitchen counter and adding the finishing touches, he called his father to wash his hands as the dinner was almost ready.

Qurban rose from the TV lounge, turned to the bathroom, and collapsed in the doorway. The young men were in shock.

They helped him stand up and led him into the kitchen. There he vomited so much blood that the sink got covered in red.

At utmost speed, the young men got a taxi to the CMH[3] in Rawalpindi. It was Sunday and there was hardly any staff. A lone senior doctor told them that there was no space and all beds were full. Muqeem pleaded with him. At last, Qurban got an injection and was sent to the PIMS.[4]

Qurban was diagnosed with a haemorrhaging stomach ulcer. The stomach was cleared of blood by a laser and tube treatment. In order to stabilize Qurban's condition, the doctors at PIMS gave him seven blood transfusions and made him stay in the hospital for ten days.

When I inquire after his health today, I get an 'okay' for an answer. When I insist, Qurban adds that he must not overstretch his body otherwise the pain will resume. Incidentally, I spot a strip of red tablets on the floor next to me. I ask no more questions.

At least those two incidents of 2009, the avalanche and his illness, have got him to quit high-portering for the time being. He was 'called' again in 2012 by a group of Pakistanis to Passu Peak. He laughs while recalling this. Obviously they had not been seriously planning to scale this seven-thousand-metre peak. They were indisposed and their equipment was ridiculous. Not even a rope was regarded as a necessary item to carry. 'They had nothing,' Qurban says. Consequently, camp 1 was the end of the adventure.

When I ask Qurban's opinion of Qudrat's climbing school, he first prevaricates a bit before getting to the point. He says that his generation, lacking any kind of education and perspective, was the one to take on the challenge of climbing. They gained a reputation and promoted their country, Pakistan. Today's young generation is being offered easier and better careers. Therefore, they are less interested in climbing, which he does not see as a bad vocation. Even so, those who turned their backs on education can resort to the chances the SMS offers them.

In order to complete Qurban's image with one more aspect, I would like to recount a little episode in which he proved to have a totally different talent: his skills as an orthopaedic expert.

In Shimshal it is not an unusual thing if, for a twisted joint or a sprained ankle, you summon a senior family member instead of the doctor Farman Ullah. The uncle will know the relevant tricks and rectify the damage. In this field, Qurban has outstanding skills. One example may be described here.

A German visitor once limped around in Shimshal with a splint on her ankle. She had sprained it back home weeks before, consulted several doctors who had fumbled about, x-rayed, and rubbed it with ointment—all without any success. A splint was the only solution the German doctors could come up with. Still, she did not want to refrain from travelling. In Shimshal, she was told that hers was a case for Qurban Mohammad. Since she had become quite weary of the futility of Western medicine, she trusted Qurban with her treatment. He hammered a strong shaft in the soil of his field. Then he tied the ankle to the shaft with a piece of cloth which he knotted speedily and effectively. He took a wedge that he had put at the ready and drove it into the shaft from above. Two or three well-measured hammer beats did the job: the ankle jerked into its proper position, having been straightened by the sudden pressure. A single howl of pain but then total incredulity and amazement! The woman could walk again and danced in jubilation for she was cured.

Notes

1. Major English-language daily newspaper in Pakistan.
2. With his son Muqeem, I later calculate the year which is 1955.
3. Civil and Military Hospital.
4. Pakistan Institute of Medical Sciences.

2.3

Sarwar Ali

High-altitude porter, born 1967

SARWAR ALI IS A SHORT, WIRY MAN, WHOM I HAVE NEVER SEEN without his baseball cap in the past ten years.

Early in the interview he seems to be a little nervous; he gesticulates and speaks with great rapidity. However, he keeps up the speed until the close of the interview. It is part of the personality of a man who, according to my interpreter Samad, is of high intelligence. Sarwar Ali has two brothers who are both well-salaried engineers. One of them works as deputy director with WAPDA[1] in Skardu. I recall that Sarwar is also a genius in growing apple and apricot trees. He says that it was his father who initiated this and taught him the ins and outs of this work.

There is more information on his schooldays than that of the previous interviewees because he belongs to a younger generation and, possibly, to a more education-orientated family. He attended only first grade in Shimshal and then moved to Gulmit. After completing junior school, his brothers made him go to Karachi. He was to earn money and contribute to financing one brother's university education. Sarwar Ali managed both—to get a job and go to school to pass his Matric exam. Afterwards, he was needed in Shimshal.

He got married in 1984. His first child, a daughter, was born in 1987. Since 1993, four sons have completed the family.

Sarwar says he took an early interest in climbing but did not make a professional start until the year 2000. Ever since, he has been a faithful partner of the tour operator ATP.

What strikes me when I compare him with my other interviewees is his modesty. Nowhere in his house do I spot photographs which show him on a mountain, and in his humble album collection there is not a single photo of Sarwar himself.

It is an incredible eight times that Sarwar Ali has been on Gasherbrum-II, and all these eight times he has not been on the top. He heartily laughs about it. It has become a running joke in Shimshal.

In my opinion, he would have definitely succeeded at least once if it was not improper for a high-altitude porter to reach the summit without any client. Also, the reasons already mentioned may contribute to his history of 'flops'. A summit bid is never without risk, and in Pakistan there is no prospect whatsoever of a reward, be it in material or immaterial form. On the other hand, Sarwar says, it remains his goal to eventually stand at the very top of Gasherbrum-II.

For his first expedition, which was arranged with ATP by his relative Qudrat Ali, Sarwar had to buy his own equipment. Although it was understood that this would be the practical test for him, he went through with it in 'Shimshali style', i.e. without specific training. Within twenty days, he climbed to Gasherbrum-II's camp 4 and thus secured his recommendation for the future. The leader of the expedition wrote a highly positive report about Sarwar's character and performance. Therefore, immediately afterwards he was allowed—or maybe ordered—by ATP to join an Italian named

Silvio on Gasherbrum-I. Thanks to Sarwar's services, Silvio made it to the top while Sarwar's highest point was camp 4.

The next two expeditions—on Broad Peak with Greeks in 2002, and on Gasherbrum-II with New Zealanders in 2003— are quickly covered in the interview. In contrast to that, the year 2004 deserves maximum recognition for it was then that he reached the summit of Nanga Parbat. It was a German-organized expedition with international members, and ATP had engaged Sarwar Ali. On this occasion, he learned why Nanga Parbat is called 'Killer Mountain'. Even on the so-called normal route—the Kinshofer Route—climbers are incessantly bombarded by falling rocks, which whiz down like cannon balls, and the danger of avalanches is always imminent. With seven of the nine members, Sarwar Ali reached the summit on 18 June as the only local climber.

In the summer of 2005, he joined an Australian expedition to Gasherbrum-II. He says that these climbers had considerable experience of climbing other eight-thousand-metre peaks in Nepal, but despite their skills and stamina, they were not meant to summit Gasherbrum-II.

The following year, Sarwar again went to his fated mountain, this time with New Zealanders. Since I know the outcome of this particular expedition, I ask some general questions, for example about the fixed ropes that commercial expeditions install on the steeper passages. How is this issue handled? Are there rules that regulate mutual contribution and assistance? He is not likely to have complete information but he knows about one important principle: the first expedition in summer fixes ropes and has the following groups pay for it or, alternatively, substitute the ropes from their own equipment. Some groups, of course, make new routes of their own. On the other hand, in crucial spots one may come across several ropes fixed by the speedier climbers so that they can pass the congestion of a slower group.[2] When an expedition is finished, it should be the rule to dismantle the total of the precious material, length by length, camp by camp, and haul the items back down. More often than not, this is neglected for various reasons. Perhaps the weather is not good enough to climb once again. Perhaps—or rather very probably—the participants and high-altitude porters are at the end of their tether and motivation, and do not feel up to scaling the mountain again for the puny reason of packing. It also happens that a camp or a fixed rope is destroyed by an avalanche, or simply buried so deeply under masses of new snow that it has to be abandoned.

In this way, a disgusting amount of garbage collects on those mountains over the years, whose ugliness is only concealed by the grace of new snow.

I also want to learn how familiar Sarwar Ali has become with Gasherbrum-II after so many expeditions. I don't really know if familiar is the right word to use here, or bored. He says that the stretch between base camp and camp 1 is by no means boring. The icefall that has to be crossed is constantly moving and that route has to be scouted anew every year. It is full of perils and by far the most difficult part of the climb. From camp 1, the routes are pretty much the same each year, and therefore he can benefit from his experience and convey it to his clients.

I am also curious to know whether expeditions bring about friendships with the clients. After all, for a couple of weeks you share happiness and sorrow, sun and blizzards, and success and failure with each other. Sarwar confirms that people are welded together on the mountain and he also exchanges e-mail addresses with them at the farewell event. A lasting association, however, will inevitably fail because there is neither telephone nor mobile or internet connection in Shimshal.

Sarwar Ali's Gasherbrum-II carousel went another round in 2006. A group from New Zealand managed to climb to a point only 35 metres short of the top but had to give up due to bad weather and health problems.

Another question that has been on my mind relates to the reception Sarwar is accorded after his adventures at the Gasherbrum-II. To the villagers, a HAP returning in one piece is all that matters. The mountain is going to be there and one can always attempt the summit bid again.

In 2007, Sarwar witnessed an operation staged by Russians on K-2 which almost had the character of a military campaign. The goal was to climb the 'King of Mountains' by an entirely new route. A camera team accompanied them and there was satellite connection with Russia where TV viewers could follow the siege of the mountain live. The plan covered three months, and they managed to follow the timeline. Sarwar says that the members included Russia's mountaineering elite. They were twenty-four climbers. Two or three of them had already scaled all Nepalese eight-thousand-metre peaks and the rest had summited at least one of them. This was clearly a promotional affair and with ambitious logistics. Upon arrival, the HAPs were contracted in written form to proceed no further than camp 1. Camp 1 onwards, the climbers planned to carry their own packs. The new route was absurdly long. Sarwar tells me that nobody has since tried it again. The very distance from base camp to Advanced Base Camp (ABC) took six to seven hours. From ABC to the top, they intended to erect no less than seven camps. The high-altitude porters' job was to carry food to camp 1, initially on a daily basis and after a month at 15-day intervals. Following a regimented schedule, the teams of five climbers set up the new camps in a seven-day rhythm. Similarly, they split into small groups and almost all members reached the summit within three days. A few of them attempted to scale K-2 in winter some four years later. The Shimshalis, Farhad Khan and Amin Ullah Baig, worked for them. It is from them that I learn that the operation was ended due to bad weather and the death of one member who contracted pneumonia.

In the summer of 2008, Sarwar Ali escorted a not-so-young couple from Italy to Gasherbrum-II. Two summit bids from camp 4 failed. Sarwar assumes that their age and lack of experience thwarted them for they had only been to the 'easy' seven-thousand-metre peaks. On this expedition, something unfortunate happened to Sarwar. He slipped on a slab of ice, took a fall, and injured his knee. It was on his own two legs that he had to drag himself to the base camp, but for the long trek on Baltoro Glacier, a horse was sent which carried him to Skardu. The doctors there did not see the need of an operation. In fact, the treatment with medicine cured him and no damage whatsoever remained.

The next year, Sarwar Ali had to attend to a single mountaineer from Iran and that also on Gasherbrum-II. When he was at camp 2, the man suddenly complained of severe pain in his abdomen, which was at first startling and inexplicable for Sarwar. Everything had to happen post-haste. In a rush, they descended to the base camp where Sarwar came to know that the Iranian had had appendicitis prior to the journey. His doctor would have preferred him to cancel the expedition. At least one of his urgent warnings had been taken to heart by the man: should the pain come back, he would have to cut short the trip immediately. Extreme cold meant deadly peril for his condition.

Sarwar does not speak at length about his expeditions in the year 2010. He only says that in this year, he was part of an international expedition under American leadership which attempted Gasherbrum-I and II, and failed on both.

In 2011, however, he met an interesting person—an elderly gentleman from Georgia (Asia)—who climbed Nanga Parbat with him. He turned out to be a member of the Georgian parliament. Sarwar describes him as supremely forthright, affable, and warm-hearted. The two of them met the same fate as all other expeditions on Nanga Parbat in the year 2011: nobody made it to the top. On the spur of the moment, the Georgian decided to go to Broad Peak with his HAP. It did not work out either, this time because of acute knee problems which forced the man to turn back. Sarwar underlines that he appreciated the alliance with the Georgian gentleman a lot. He even felt a kind of friendship between them. He had been quite generous with the tip as well.

In 2012, Sarwar Ali embarked on his eighth trip to Gasherbrum-II with three Germans, three Australians, one Italian, and one Swede. Since the outcome is already determined (the never-ending snowfall prevented them from any major climbing activity), I am more interested in knowing a bit more about the atmosphere in the camps—if moods are dampened every morning upon the first glance out the tent door, if participants gradually hang their heads, or if frustration casts its dark shadows on the team spirit leading people to fight? Sarwar's answer to all of these questions is in the negative. He says that all of his expedition members bravely kept their good spirits and told themselves that failure was not brought about by their lack of skills but by the malevolence of the weather.

When I inquire about the SMS, Sarwar says that it is not

being utilized sufficiently. He also questions the qualification of certain younger climbing instructors. According to him, their performance is not exactly impeccable and they make mistakes. Altogether, the institution lacks a concrete agenda.

At the close of the interview, Sarwar Ali expresses a view that I would not naturally have expected of a high-altitude porter. With regard to the younger generation, he says that they should comprehend and internalize that climbing can also be a meaningful and worthwhile activity, pursued without any material benefit.

Notes

1. Water and Power Development Authority.
2. Fixed ropes have been mentioned in Meherban Shah's chapter as well.

2.4

Meherban Shah

High-altitude porter, born around 1957

LIKE HIS WIFE JAMILA—WHO I MEET EVERY YEAR IN SHUWERTH on the Shimshal Pass—Meherban Shah is always cheerful. He radiates happiness and likes to joke with others, except when the subject is his son Ghulam Ali Shah's death on Sonia Peak in 2001.

Meherban Shah is of slender build and, at first glance, comes across as younger than his 55 years. However, his gait and posture betray this impression. He seems to walk with aching hips, his upper body assuming a pain-avoiding position. It is wheat-cutting season and the hard work plagues him all the more.

At the beginning of the interview, the general idea of alpine climbing comes up and Meherban Shah pronounces a surprising thing: the Shimshalis did not take to mountaineering and climbing until their encounter with Francis Younghusband. Born in 1863, Francis Younghusband, from the 1880s to 1907, was one of the key players in the so-called Great Game (the competition between the colonial power Great Britain and the Empire of the Russian Czar for supremacy in Central Asia). As described by Peter Hopkirk in his book *The Great Game* (London 1990), Younghusband's fascinating personality combined the characters of a researcher and explorer, officer, pioneer, spy, and youthful adventurer. In 1889, Younghusband was on a mission to locate the infamous Shimshal Pass because some unwelcome things were happening there. With exasperating frequency, merchants were being raided and plundered, and it was mostly on the orders of the ruler of Hunza, Safdar Ali, that these hold-ups were performed.

Up there at almost 4,700 metres, a memorable encounter between the young Briton and the Shimshalis materialized. It started with a prank that the villagers played on him. For a moment it made him jump in fear and terror. Hopkirk in his book, and Younghusband in his notes, depict the roguish humour of those former Shimshalis in a way which reveals that their great-great-grandchildren today have inherited their genes.

I think that Meherban's hypothesis is based on a movie, which was made in Hunza and Gulkin in 1996 by a Russian director, in which Rajab Shah, Meherban Shah, and Tafat Shah participated. It was not the lead roles that these Shimshalis had to play; rather they were hired as climbing experts who, for example, fixed ropes. The film may have indicated that in the nineteenth century the British were the forerunners of mountaineering. This could be the reason why Meherban sees the illustrious protagonist of the Great Game, Francis Younghusband, as the one who imparted the idea of climbing to his village.

When I ask him how long he attended school, he laughs and replies in Wakhi, 'kam, kam', meaning 'very little'. This could be for a period of one year maximum. The teacher was Ghulam Sultan, as for all Shimshalis of his generation.

Meherban Shah had occasionally joined trekking groups as a porter but had never dreamt of expeditions. This changed in

1991 when Rajab Shah—who had already gained experience—
encouraged him to try working as a high-altitude porter on a
Japanese tour to the seven-thousand-metre peak of Momil Sar.
Meherban highlights how ignorant and unskilled he had been
until the moment Rajab Shah gave him crampons, karabiners,
and a piece of string, and taught him the basics of climbing.
What followed was full-scale success. All of the six Japanese
members plus the three Shimshali high porters (Tafat Shah
had also joined Rajab Shah and Meherban Shah) reached
the summit of this 7,343 metre peak which, according to
Meherban, is quite hazardous between camps 1 and 3.

In 1992, it was once again a group of six Japanese
mountaineers who hired Meherban as a HAP on Gasherbrum-
II. Rajab Shah and a Pakistani guide named Nazir Sabir also
accompanied him. Meherban says that when they risked a
summit bid from camp 4, the already biting wind increased
into a dramatic blizzard. In such a situation, they could
only turn back and descend to the base camp. Nazir Sabir
actually offered two of his Shimshali partners to try again,
this time without the Japanese. Thus it happened that not a
single expedition member but three locals stood on the top
of Gasherbrum-I. According to Meherban, the Japanese were
perfectly satisfied with their services. At the debriefing in the
Ministry of Tourism, they wrote them favourable certificates.

In the year 1993, Meherban Shah built a new house
in Farmanabad and could not afford a period of absence.
His friend Rajab Shah is the first person to have taken up
permanent residence in the new settlement Farmanabad.

Cooperation with Nazir Sabir, who had been a tour operator
since 1988, continued in the summer of 1994. The expedition
included Japanese climbers this time as well, and the peak
chosen was Shispare (7,619 metres). With a lot of emphasis

and alternating between Wakhi and English, Meherban tries to illustrate the perniciousness of this mountain when he says 'too much dangerous'. The mountain has rock faces with no layer of snow or ice which are continuously being hit by rockfall. He extols the skills and stamina of the Japanese in the eternally bad weather. In contrast, the Japanese food in base camp gets bad marks in his memory: 'too much rice, only rice!'

On 13 August 1995, when six climbers died on K-2 due to its infamous changes in the weather pattern, Meherban Shah and Rajab Shah were working for a Dutch team on the same mountain. There were eleven Dutch and six HAPs: two from Hunza, two Baltis, and two Shimshalis.

They had managed to reach camp 4, just below the Bottleneck, when the worst-case scenario occured: there was no rope left to secure this crucial stretch on K-2!

Meherban describes the organization and logistics of fixed ropes in a different way than Sarwar Ali. He says one team alone can hardly bring along the bulk of ropes for the whole distance from base camp to the summit. The various teams cooperate and divide the distance into parts. However, relying blindly on previous agreements may be precarious, and this is what happened to Meherban and his Dutch friends: they looked into the void. No previous group had fixed any ropes above camp 4. The weather was good and descending was not an option.

They wondered if they should start a hit-or-miss action and cling to withering hopes for an old rope from the previous year. Ultimately, they settled for taking the risk. They began at 3 a.m. and it was worth a try. Not only did they dig up a rope from under the snow, but there was an ice axe sticking out near the route, abandoned or lost by whomsoever in whatever kind of distress. It was under these circumstances that the

Dutch and Shimshali climbers made it to the summit of K-2 after struggling for nineteen hours through waist-deep snow. The only person to have used supplementary oxygen was Rainer, the Dutch expedition leader. Meherban says that it was 10 p.m. when he and Rajab Shah came back to camp 4 in a totally exhausted state. The other two arrived at midnight.

Meherban Shah's next climb, in the summer of 1996, was an expedition to Passu Peak with an exclusively Pakistani team, organized by the Alpine Club of Pakistan. Seven Shimshalis, among them Rajab Shah, Aziz Baig, Hazil Shah, and Meherban Shah, participated as regular members and not as high-altitude porters. The rest of the group members, numbering twenty according to Meherban (fifty-eight according to Hazil Shah), were predominantly from Lahore and seemed to be quite amateur climbers. Hazil was a novice as well. Small wonder then that he fell in a crevasse twice on the difficult stretch between camp 1 and camp 2, and had to be pulled out of it by his Shimshali companions in lengthy operations. However, Hazil and all of his Shimshali counterparts managed to reach the top of the 7,478 metre-high Passu Peak while none of the other members succeeded.

In 1997, Pakistan celebrated its Golden Jubilee—fifty years of independence and the foundation of the Islamic Republic of Pakistan. This occasion was marked in the field of mountaineering too. It had to be nothing short of Mount Everest—the world's highest mountain—that was to be conquered by Pakistan's climbing elite. Besides two Baltis, Colonel Sher Khan and the leader Nazir Sabir, these elite mountaineers also included the two Shimshalis, Rajab Shah and Meherban Shah. Both of them have related the story of this memorable flop. Their accounts complement each other so I am telling the Everest story here from both perspectives simultaneously.

Independent of each other, both men emphasize how 'easy' Mount Everest is in comparison to K-2 and Nanga Parbat. Meherban claims that only a short passage is moderately dangerous. His overall conclusion is that 'it's nothing!'

The two also imply that they felt superior to Nazir Sabir in terms of climbing skills and that they would have made it to the summit if it had not been for the orders of their expedition leader.

Meherban says Nazir Sabir had been exhausted upon his arrival at the highest camp before the summit bid. The leader was of the opinion that the high-altitude storm raging in the death zone was too strong to risk an attempt at climbing.

According to Rajab Shah, they would have reached the summit by 7 a.m. if they had started well before dawn and kept up a good pace. They would not have been thwarted by the high-altitude gales that typically commence between 8 and 9 a.m. However, permission for an early start was denied by Nazir Sabir. He issued the order for a late departure and that too had to be a collective enterprise. The two Shimshalis comment on this order in a level-headed way and in retrospect do not display any disappointment or bitterness towards Nazir Sabir. All they say is that they started too late and were too slow to make it to the summit. It does not matter if they weren't successful.

Three years later, Nazir Sabir became the first Pakistani ever to arrive at the very top of Everest, which hugely increased his reputation. Rajab Shah and Meherban Shah call him a good friend. They respect his accomplishments. He has also thrived as a businessman due to his knowledge of the English language, and as chairman of the Alpine Club of Pakistan, and has even started a political career by utilizing his popularity.

In 1998, Meherban joined one of the two Japanese expeditions on Gasherbrum-II mentioned in Qurban Mohammad's chapter, and reached the summit along with several climbers.

A year later, on Broad Peak, he had to learn what it means for a high-altitude porter to be dependent on as well as be responsible for an ambitious, self-willed, and inflexible climber. Personal responsibility is by no means the part of a HAP's job. Still, it does happen that the paying client who manages to survive by the breadth of a hair but gets severely frostbitten, blames his high-altitude porter for laxity and negligence. This happened on K-2 in 2008.

The Frenchman Hugues d'Aubarède, who was to die nine years later in 2008, was obsessed with the summit of Broad Peak. In high camp, Meherban had warned him and his female companion that the weather was about to change. He told them that it was foolish to insist on a summit bid; that the stakes would be higher than they are when humans are at lower altitudes. D'Aubarède remained stubborn. The outcomes that followed were exactly what Meherban had predicted. In the raging wind and snowfall, they were hardly able to move. Progress was desperately slow. However, not even during this ordeal: shivering from cold, exposed to the fury of the elements, and inconceivably distant from any rescue option, did the Frenchman hesitate in his intention. It was after nightfall when they arrived on the summit.

They lost their orientation while descending. Meherban's face still reflects the fear and despondency that beset him when he stumbled around and searched for camp 4 while d'Aubarède and the woman were forced to stand and wait in one spot. When—more or less by coincidence—he discovered the tents in the blizzard, he was relieved beyond words. However, he still had to collect the two individuals out there and escort them down to the camp. Meherban is not sure if it was from cold, fear, or the shock of relief but as d'Aubarède staggered behind him, he was utterly tight-lipped.

Only later, on the way to the base camp did he open his mouth and uttered words of gratitude for Meherban's vigilance and care. Miraculously, they had escaped without frostbite.

The next expedition, organized by ATP in 2000 with one female and two male climbers from Spain, took Meherban Shah to K-2 once again. On the whole, they spent four weeks on the slopes but, although the team was strong (he extols the woman but can't recall her name), the weather thwarted their ambitions with too much new snow. They had pitched the high camp at 8,200 metres, directly below the Bottleneck, and waited for two nights. This meant challenging fate in a threefold way: first of all, at this altitude the human body rapidly depletes its resources, and recovering them right there is impossible. Second, the risk of avalanches is high in this area. Third, they had run out of food. This necessitated the speediest descent. Within two days, they managed to reach the safety of base camp.

In 2001, it was once again a Spanish group that hired Meherban and K-2 was their destination—this time with another Shimshali, Jehan Baig. There were even more parallels with the previous year, for instance, they had a one-month sojourn on the mountain, established camp 4 below the Bottleneck, failed on the summit bid, and the food ran out. Meherban's comment on the latter is that this is almost 'normal' on expeditions. As long as the goodies are there, they will be devoured—mostly in the lower camps—and rations for later will not be spared.

However, what embedded the 2001 K-2 expedition inextinguishably on Meherban's memory was the message from Shimshal that reached him in the base camp. This was the news of his son's death.

Ghulam Ali Shah, his eldest son, had been killed by an avalanche on Sonia Peak[1] along with another young Shimshali. The team was deeply shocked. Condolences were expressed from all sides, including army captain Iqbal who was to meet his own death on K-2 a few years later.[2]

All of a sudden I feel that Meherban has become tired of the interview and my endless questions. His answers are getting shorter; he also seems distracted at times. He wants to put an end to the conversation. And who would grudge him that?

Meherban Shah went to K-2 an incredible four times more, in 2002 (with Americans), 2004 (with Koreans), 2005 (with Iranians), and 2008 (with Singaporeans). The scaling of the summit remained an unachieved goal though. On all four expeditions, Jehan Baig was with him. In the disastrous summer of 2008, Meherban returned to Shimshal after completing his expedition, whereas Jehan Baig and the young Meherban Karim agreed to go for another job (with Hugues d'Aubarède) which ended with their deaths.

In 2006, Meherban Shah was on the summit of Broad Peak for the second time along with five Spaniards. Two other summit bids of the eight-thousand-metre peaks should be recorded here: Gasherbrum-I in 2004, Gasherbrum-II in 2010, and finally Passu Peak in 2011.

'Now, I have finished,' he says this in 2012. His two sons— one is a soldier, the other works in Sost as a driver for a

Chinese employer—thought that it was high time their father quit. They no longer need support from him.

From 1991 to 2011, he has spent each summer on expeditions with only three exceptions. In his accomplishments on the five Pakistani eight-thousand-metre peaks, only Nanga Parbat is missing although he was twice on Broad Peak. In fact, he has had his four eight-thousand-metre peaks painted on the walls of his house by a Shimshali artist.

A different kind of success and an annually recurring one is his orchard in Farmanabad. Besides numerous sorts of apples and apricots, he can even harvest cherries. Last but not the least, Meherban Shah has been an active member of the Ismaili Volunteers for many years.

Notes

1. C. F. Hazil Shah's account of his Sonia Peak expedition.
2. See in Amruddin's chapter.

2.5

Farhad Khan

High-altitude porter, born 1959

WHEREAS MY PREVIOUS INTERVIEWEES CAN BE DESCRIBED
as having wiry or slight builds, Farhad Khan is taller and
heavily built. Similar to Sarwar Ali, he staunchly shadows
his face with a baseball cap. He refrains from being loud and
cheerful, and showing big gestures. He seems to be quite
impassive and self-controlled.

His calmness makes his answers a bit colourless and
anaemic. An antithesis to his unshakeable composure will be
Hazil Shah's blooming verbosity in the next chapter.

There is a TV set in Farhad's house which is something
that can be found in increasing numbers in Shimshali
households. He does not have any photo collections. Two
mementos is all he can show me. The first is a 2006 edition of
a French alpine magazine which focuses on the Karakorums
and Shimshal, and contains a photo of him. The other is an
accumulation of hundreds of tiny, wildly confused photos
which a Japanese had printed as a book after his 2005 K-2
expedition, and sent to Farhad Khan. I thumb through it in
growing bewilderment. The collection is a jumble of gaudy
little pictures without any captions, encompassing all kinds
of subjects and not just green meadows and high-camp tents.

It has portraits of people posturing with their ice axes, but also bleached-out parts of dead bodies in the snow.

Farhad Khan attended school at a time when Daulat Amin conducted his classes in the open air or in hay sheds. After completing the sixth class, he spent two more years in Gulmit where he could live with relatives. It is from him that I learn that during his childhood in the 1960s, the traditional homemade woollen clothes were gradually replaced by the Pakistani national attire, shalwar kameez.

In the 1970s, Farhad suffered from a strange pain in his left calf. The doctors in Gilgit could not identify the reason. He had to travel to Karachi and be examined by experts in the Aga Khan University Hospital. They diagnosed an obstruction of the blood flow in his veins. It was cured through an operation and he has been fine since.

Farhad Khan is among those HAPs who took to climbing later in their lives. He had a specific motive too. For a long time, he was busy in the construction of the link road from Passu to Shimshal. His was a crucial job as he worked with the compressor. This job ended in 2003 and it might be the cause of his partial loss of hearing. With that, he has served the community in an extraordinary way but he does not even talk about it.

In the same year, Farhad switched to high-portering and went on his first expedition. He emphasises that he does this job just to make money so his four children can get the best possible education. If he could get the necessary means in a less backbreaking and hazardous way, he would quit tomorrow.

In 2003, Farhad participated in a three-day climbing training on Malangutti Glacier which was conducted by Rajab Shah. The equipment came from the stocks of Rajab, Qudrat

Ali, and Shaheen Baig. The 'students'—among whom was
Amin Ullah Baig as well—had to take turns.

Farhad's first expedition was on the lesser known seven-
thousand-metre peak, Gasherbrum-5. He says that the
eighteen members of the expedition belonged to the privileged
classes. They were doctors and pilots of different nationalities.
Even before arriving at camp 2, the route seemed too
dangerous for them. Farhad assumes that too much may have
been at stake for such VIPs in terms of jobs and careers. In
any case, they refused to take risks and ended the expedition
at camp 1.

In the year 2004, the Golden Jubilee of the first ascent of
K-2 was celebrated. Farhad Khan had been hired as a high-
altitude porter by a climber from Iran for an expedition to
K-2. The manner in which he reports the event still mirrors
his consternation. At this festive occasion, the hordes of
mountaineers arriving from across the world must have been
beyond description. Upon arrival at camp 2 (6,400m), he and
the Iranian faced a sea of tents and failed to find some space
for their own. This discouraged the Iranian from climbing any
further. How was he supposed to negotiate the Bottleneck in
the midst of such crowds? Farhad does not regret the decision
to turn back. He says he had some problems with the altitude
and was glad to escape the bustle.

Then in 2005, along with five Japanese, he was again on
K-2 for two months altogether. He hauled 16 kg up to an
elevation of 8,100 metres where they pitched the tents of
camp 4. Here the group's interpreter (the Japanese did not
speak English) revealed to Farhad that this was his terminus
and the summit bid was taboo for him.

He did not hide his disappointment. He was angry
because the weather was good and there was hardly any risk

of avalanches. He is convinced that he would have reached the summit. Of the Japanese, two climbers—a woman of 22 and a man of 24 years—reached the top with the help of supplementary oxygen. Farhad frankly admits that they descended in a state of wordlessness. He did not have the smallest exchange with them because his annoyance at the missed summit was too strong.

In 2006, Farhad Khan was sent to Muztagh Ata by ATP. Muztagh Ata is a 7,546-metre peak just across the Chinese border, and it is considered to be an 'easy' seven-thousand-metre peak.

This time again, he failed to reach the top because both of his clients were wearing low-quality shoes. He says that they started 'too early' on summit day. This sounds absurd, but it isn't. Muztagh Ata is climbed on a route facing north-west where the sun appears extremely late, which means that the climbers at over 6,800 metres have to survive in freezing temperatures until the sun helps to thaw the stiff extremities. This can be managed if the climbers walk at a smooth pace and wear well insulated boots. According to Farhad, both of these climbers were in bad shape as well. They were creeping along in the manner of snails and complained of frostbite in their toes. Indeed, the morning temperature was in the double digits below zero. Farhad obviously had to turn back with them, although he could have easily covered the home stretch.

Farhad also mentions the colossal K-2 siege by twenty-four Russian elite climbers in the summer of 2007. Sarwar Ali has also talked about it in the previous chapter; however, Farhad's report is comparatively laconic. He attests the exceptional climbing skills of the Russians but says that only eleven of them made it to the summit. He recalls that four members

suffered from frostbite and had to be flown back to Russia
ahead of time.

The summer of 2008 was fatal for Shimshalis. During
this time, Farhad Khan was on K-2 with a group of five
French and Italian climbers. They spent six weeks on the
mountain. When they had successfully erected camp 3 and
were ready for the climb to camp 4 and the summit, a
19-day period of bad weather set in. This meant sitting
idly in the base camp, listening to the rattling tent fabric,
shovelling snow, and managing the thinning food supplies.
When they packed in disappointment and started the trek
back to Skardu, the sun showed up again. However, it
seemed like a total eclipse when Farhad learned of Jehan
Baig and Meherban Karim's death.

Farhad describes his unsuccessful summit attempts in a
succinct manner. Listening to all of these accounts makes me
conclude that he did have a very strong desire to stand on top
of an eight-thousand-metre peak, regardless of the dangers
and obstacles. However, this desire was not to be fulfilled
until three years later.

In 2009, Farhad became acquainted with an American
called Fabrizio, who was the owner of a company specializing
in mountain travel, and was working in cooperation with ATP.
The man planned an expedition on Broad Peak with sixteen
members. Six of them had additionally secured a permit for
K-2. For Farhad, this meant a job of two months altogether
on two different mountains, whose base camps are in the
immediate vicinity of each other. Unfortunately, neither on
Broad Peak nor on K-2 did they go any further than camp 3
due to a shortage of time, says Farhad Khan.

The following year Fabrizio intended to go on a similar
double expedition. Fourteen climbers came on board for

Broad Peak, three of whom aspired to summit K-2 afterwards. The outcome of this expedition resembles that of the last one: the climbers reached camp 3 on Broad Peak; on K-2, they had to give up between camps 3 and 4.

When I talk to him about the loads that the HAPs are allocated, Farhad basically confirms that the issue is handled arbitrarily but, in his own case, was managed in a fair manner. He says that between base camp and camp 1, a pack of 20 kg is 'permitted' but the limit is never maxed out. Scales are rarely applied and it is by pure guesswork that the loads for the individual high porters are assembled. His friend, Fabrizio, always tried to give a little more weight to the expedition members rather than going to the limit with the HAPs.

In 2011, after eight years of merciless labour, Farhad did finally reach the summit of an eight-thousand-metre peak. He scaled the summit of Broad Peak. He still remembers that on the summit day, a formidable thirty-five climbers started from camp 4, out of whom only four made it to the summit. Farhad says that he spent twenty-five days on the mountain and refrains from sharing further details.

He talks about the summer of 2012 in a sparse manner. This time the expedition had set off for Broad Peak with three Spaniards included; however, bad weather forced the climbers to descend from camp 3.

Farhad Khan joined one winter expedition as well. This was the Russians' K-2 tour in December 2011, which I will describe in Amin Ullah Baig's chapter. From Farhad, I only learn that one of the Russians died of pneumonia.

Farhad is a person of few words and doesn't seem interested in sharing more details. He plans to continue high-portering until all his children have completed their education. His focus and determination is clearly bearing fruit. His eldest son has acquired a BBA degree, works with an insurance company, and earns good money. The second son studies at a college in Rawalpindi, while the younger two, a son and a daughter, attend a high school in Gilgit. Farhad Khan, therefore, can easily count the years that remain until he can quit signing up for these expeditions.

2.6

Hazil (Hasil) Shah

High-altitude porter and businessman, born 1972

HAZIL SHAH IS AN ENERGETIC MAN WHOSE WAISTLINE HAS
slightly expanded over the past few years. I have known him
for a long time but merely in his role as a businessman in
any likely enterprise, be it as a buyer of Chinese iron stoves
or as the founder and manager of a hotel. Some blame him
for charging extravagant prices for accommodation and
food, while others call him a great fellow. Opinions about
him are divided.

The fact remains that Hazil has the most exciting stories
to tell. What needs to be seen is whether these are true
or not.

When he talks, he relives all his scenes with suitable facial
expressions and body language. He is a master of rhetoric. He
lowers his voice to a whisper when he wants to convey drama;
he pauses like a professional before a punch line. In short, he
knows how to fascinate his listeners.

Before I interviewed him, I had other Shimshalis tell me
a few things about his recent (and not-so-recent) business
dealings and transactions—the scope of which is impressive.
It could be because, as an orphan, he had to start early on
to make money, and of course he has some innate sense of

business. Hazil Shah is excellent at identifying sources and utilizing opportunities of increasing his income.

He likes to travel across the 4,934-metre-high Khunjerab Pass into Kashgar (China), in order to buy all sorts of merchandise, which he can sell at profitable rates in Shimshal. These include solar-powered batteries, sleeping bags, sunglasses, leather jackets, and even used shoes.

His attempt at entering the tourism sector as a tour operator, and his latest project of opening a tourist lodge in Shimshal have already been mentioned.

What entitles him to appear in this book is his job as a high-altitude porter or, as he likes to put it, a 'tour guide'. Incidentally, he speaks reasonably good English so Samad can lean back and listen.

During his school years, Hazil was quite a character and loved to provoke and make fun of his classmates. His pranks spiced up Daulat Amin's teaching. Like most of my interviewees, Hazil was taught nothing but Urdu and Science in his first six years of school. English classes started as late as in class seven, at first merely in the shape of the ABC, which they had to chant in chorus.

Both of Hazil's parents died during his childhood—his father when he was six, his mother when he was ten. With his three sisters (only one of whom is still alive today), he grew up in his uncle Mohammad Ullah's family.

In 1985, at 13 years of age, Hazil decided to run away to Karachi. This city is 1,600 kilometres south of Shimshal. He confided in his best friend Mehboob and made him pledge to keep mum for two full days so he would not be found out and nabbed on his escape. In Shimshal, if a child disappears for one or two nights, it does not cause much concern; everybody knows that the kid is sleeping in a relative's house. After he had trusted Mehboob with his school bag on the day of his departure, Hazil, with 700 rupees in his pocket that his late mother had given him, marched the 55-km distance to Passu in two days. He spent the night at Ziarat[1], which used to be a shelter for all Shimshali travellers. It offered him a fireplace and a pile of quilts for comfort.

In Passu, the young fugitive knocked on the door of his mother's sister. She would have appreciated it if he had stayed with her and continued school there. He did not tell her his true intentions but quietly vanished early the next morning, first to Gilgit by bus for 20 rupees, and from there to Rawalpindi, where his uncle Mohammad Ullah was based with the army, for 85 rupees.

Meanwhile, his disappearance had been noticed in Shimshal and people had started a search. Within a day, relatives hurried to Passu but could not find him. They moved onwards to Gilgit but he wasn't there either, and then they looked at the passenger list of NATCO.[2] They found an entry of his name and immediately figured out that he was sitting in the bus to Rawalpindi.

They grabbed the phone and announced the runaway to Uncle Mohammad. He immediately reached the bus station and caught his nephew. Mohammad suggested that Hazil stay in Pindi but he couldn't break the child's obstinacy: 'No, no, I am going. [It is] good for me.' After a while, Mohammad Ullah admitted defeat. He gave his nephew some more money and bade farewell to him. According to Hazil Shah, the entire journey of 1,600-km to Karachi cost him 400 rupees.

He remained without a job for a week in Karachi. Then he approached the job centre of the local Ismaili community and explained his situation to them. He could soon start an office job in which he would work during the day. Simultaneously, he attended an evening school. His hard work was rewarded when he successfully completed his tenth grade.

When he returned to Shimshal, Uncle Mohammad began to press him for marriage. Hazil laughs and tells us that his uncle had already selected a bride. In this way, Hazil became a husband at the tender age of seventeen. However, it took awfully long until a baby arrived at his home. After a futile wait of years, they decided to embark upon the long journey to Karachi for medical treatment. It was to be a sojourn of several years. The medical skills at the Aga Khan University Hospital bore the desired fruit: a daughter and two sons were born by Caesarean sections.

Hazil Shah started as an ordinary porter with trekking groups and gradually climbed the social ladder to the position of a high-altitude porter.

In 1992, he met three Germans in Passu and asked if they were interested in climbing Mingli Sar with him. He says that Mingli Sar was not difficult at that time; even crampons were not required, and a rope was the only thing needed to cross one big and one small crevasse. As yet, he has climbed Mingli Sar at least seven times. He says he was taught how to climb by experienced mountaineers from the USA, England, and Italy, whom he joined as a porter. Later, he also participated in a training organized by Rajab Shah on Malangutti Glacier.

In the year 1996, Hazil joined the big expedition to Passu Peak that was led by Rajab Shah and Meherban Shah. The members of the Alpine Club of Pakistan doubted his skills. They thought that he was inexperienced and would not be able to keep pace with the professional climbers on such a difficult mountain. He told them that if Rajab Shah and Meherban Shah could do it, he would certainly do it too as he was both young and strong. They relented and gave him the chance. He forgets to mention that he had to be pulled out from two crevasses.[3] Some of the participants, according to Hazil, did not venture beyond advanced base camp; ninety per cent gave up at camp 1. In the end, only seven climbers arrived at the summit—all of them Shimshalis—including Hazil Shah.

In August of that year, Hazil had a job with seven Frenchmen on Spantik. His colleague on this tour was Aman Khan, Rajab Shah's eldest son, who died in an accident three years later. When the team had reached camp 3, the weather began to look unreliable, which quickly dispirited all members, except one.

This man confided in Hazil that the opportunity was too good to waste. He told Hazil that both of them must try and go. The man further said, 'I offer you extra cash, but keep your mouth shut until we are off.' Although the last passage on Spantik is long, they succeeded. 'Like clockwork', Hazil says, the Frenchman walked, and after summitting they even descended to camp 2.

In 1997, he was hired as a HAP by an Iranian group on Gasherbrum-II. The mention of this particular experience makes him go silent. It looks like he is about to utter something much unexpected. It turns out that several expedition teams were on the slopes of Gasherbrum-II, including one from America as well. The Iranians forbade Hazil to speak to them. He wasn't even allowed to greet them, or to say 'hi' to them.

Later, something outlandish happened to him near the summit. Shortly before the very last metres of the climb, Hazil felt thirsty and took his thermos bottle from out of his pack. While doing this, he inadvertently pulled out one of the two little flags that Shimshali high-altitude porters always carry with them: the Pakistani flag and the red-and-green one of the Ismaili denomination. The Iranians saw this and instantly radioed to the expedition leader at base camp. Hazil did not understand anything as they were talking in Persian. After speaking to the expedition leader, they yelled at him and said, 'Don't you dare climb to the summit with us. This is an order.' And indeed, while they were cheering up there and posing for photos, they did not let him come near them or reach the top.

Two Germans were watching the entire scene of the Iranians denouncing, verbally abusing, and threatening Hazil. They took him under their wing and told him that he could join them to the summit if he so wished. Hazil agreed, and it was with the Germans that he returned to camp 4 where they spent the night as they were too tired to pack up and continue descending.

Hazil, however, was gripped by the fear of his own team and wanted to avoid any contact with them. 'I immediately started the Shimshali walk,' he says. This means that he continued his descent at a rapid pace, with neither a friend nor an enemy. Besides fear, he now felt growing exasperation and fury. The scene on the summit kept recurring in his mind. He was so absorbed in his thoughts that he forgot about everything around him. For a long time he did not even notice that he was walking bare-headed. At dusk, he had reached camp 2 but continued to descend stubbornly, blind from rage. He knew that the Iranians' doctor was staying in camp 1. He had decided that he would report the whole story to the doctor. After a while, his head started aching from cold and he noticed that his ears were half frozen from the icy winds. Almost in a panic, he jerked his backpack from his shoulders and rummaged for his cap, but it wasn't there. He must have lost it in his bafflement, or hidden it in an unaccustomed place.

He arrived at camp 1 in the small hours and collapsed with

exhaustion. The tents were dark and stood there soundless and shut. With his cries for help, he managed to wake the doctor up, who opened the mess tent for him. Unfortunately, Hazil was so flattened physically and emotionally that he was unable to answer the doctor's questions. And then he did something that totally bewildered the poor man and made him drop what little sympathy and compassion he had left for the wretched fellow. Hazil unzipped his jacket and out fell the cap from an inner pocket. A fit of madness seized him. He grabbed his ice axe and hacked the cap in pieces, while cursing immoderately. The doctor feared for his dear life and escaped.

Later, when the Iranian members arrived in base camp, they punished Hazil Shah by ignoring him. Not a single word was exchanged between them. There happened to be an army captain at base camp who was Ismaili and spoke Farsi too. He walked straight to the Iranian tents to demand an explanation for their behaviour. Hazil says that the effort bore no fruit. After the expedition was over, he went to the Ministry of Tourism in Islamabad to report the affair and complain about how he had been humiliated by the Iranians.

In Qurban Mohammad and Meherban Shah's chapters, the two Japanese expeditions conducted on Gasherbrum-II in 1998 were mentioned. Hazil Shah took part in the one that was accompanied by a team of the TV channel NHK. What he describes is a mammoth event. According to him, more than one-thousand porters had been hired for the trip to base camp. For the twenty-two expedition members, no fewer than eleven cooks were at work. As a high porter, he physically experienced what it meant to make a complex movie. Not only did he have to haul the heavy camera, the tripod, and the batteries, for the sake of good scenes and in order to capture 'drama' and 'action' convincingly, he had to climb both behind and ahead of the protagonists. Downright hazardous were the camera positions which he had to seek out to catch the best possible perspective. Additionally, he reached the summit of Gasherbrum-II. However, this is denied by his cousin Ali Musa. Hazil underlines the good cooperation with the Japanese. He says that he has a couple of appreciative certificates in his files in Islamabad.

Before he moves on to the year 1999, Hazil's face assumes an expression of solemnity and momentousness. When he starts to speak, his voice clearly sounds distinguished. The strategic pauses he makes in his speech contribute to the greatness of what he is saying: '1999, K-2. I working with Hans Kammerlander.[4] He is very nice man, very strong, very good friend, very good partner. I make route, everything is cleared.'

Of course Hazil knows the reason why, in 1999, Hans did not climb from camp 4 to the summit of K-2, despite the best possible conditions. Since it's a 'secret', I must switch off the cassette recorder. He makes me swear to keep mum on what he is about to tell me. After he has whispered to me the improbable secret about which Hans had confided him up there, I shake my head in disbelief. Simultaneously I decide to check on this information when I am back home in Germany. (I did so. I phoned his secretary and upon querying Kammerlander, she called back and said Hans did not know the name Hazil Shah).

The cassette recorder is switched on again when Hazil ends his story. With his friend Hans, he later went from K-2 base camp to Payu (which is at least four trekking days on the Baltoro trip) nonstop and arrived at 1 p.m. Hazil says that a bottle of Coca Cola was 600 rupees in that year, and Hans bought one for each of them.

In the summer of 2000, Hazil was on Gasherbrum-II again. He worked for three Austrians, a father and his two sons: Rainer, Gerfried, and Wolfgang Göschl. The two young men were a strong pair and did everything without high porters. It was the father, formerly quite a remarkable climber, whom Hazil was to join for the summit bid. However, prior to the last stage, Rainer lost heart and said, 'Let it be, Hazil. I am too tired. You did a great job and I am glad to have made it up to here.' Both of the sons, of course, succeeded in reaching the top.

Gerfried was especially strong. Hazil calls him his 'good friend Gerfried'. Suddenly he becomes sombre and points to a German-language newspaper article which he has pinned onto the cupboard in his restaurant. The headline reads, 'Gerfried is dead.' I learn that in the winter of 2011–12, he was on Gasherbrum-I along with the Swiss Cedric Hählen and the Pakistani Nissar Sadpara. All three of them disappeared without a trace.

Actually, Hazil's own biography was traumatic for him. Only gradually did he recover from it. The physical effects alone took years to abate. It was the fatal expedition to Sonia Peak in 2001 that has been engraved on Shimshal's collective memory.

A Frenchman had come to Shimshal with his guide Ishaq Ali from North Pakistan Adventure, planning to climb the six-thousand-metre high Sonia Peak, which lies at a distance of at least a five-day trek from Shimshal. It was already rather late in the year. The man hired several Shimshalis as porters and Hazil Shah, according to himself, as a climbing guide. Hazil says that the familiar route on the mountain was long and cumbersome. 'I make new route,' a shorter and safer one, in his opinion. With one high camp, the team reached the summit quite straightforwardly. On the same day, snowfall began and it did not stop for three whole days. It wasn't an ordinary thing in the autumn season.

While the snowfall continued, the group had to traverse a slope towards Chafchingol Pass. Hazil assures me that prior to departure, he had instructed them that a maximum of five people could go together. Any higher number of climbers was likely to trigger an avalanche. His own group made the start. They had to break trail through breast-deep snow. Visibility was next to zero.

Hazil suspects that the others did not follow his orders. They went in larger numbers.

Then, suddenly, his group was hit by an avalanche. It had developed in a matter of seconds. Behind Hazil was Ghulam Ali Shah, Meherban Shah's eldest son, who carried one of the heavy blue expedition drums. The 20-kg container, along with its porter, was spun around by the force of the avalanche, pummelling Hazil as well. He can't tell how often he was hit because he lost consciousness. His guess is that he was buried in the snow masses for fifteen to twenty minutes until he succeeded in clawing and digging his way out with the force of desperation.

He looked around and found no trace of the other four members of his group. In a panic, he began digging for them. He does not tell me where the rest of the group lingered. He found two of his companions—Jehan Baig and his younger brother Ejaz Karim—alive. Hazil was spitting blood now, but he still helped the two injured ones to get rid of the snow that had filled their mouths. In the draft of the avalanche they had gasped for oxygen like drowning men, and the powder-like snow had plugged their mouths and noses.

But they were alive.

Ghulam Ali Shah and Ezat Mohammad, two hopeful young men, could only be retrieved dead.

At some point, the rest of the climbers, including the Frenchman, must have arrived at the scene. Again, Hazil does not say much about them, except this: none of them was willing to take the hike into Koksil to organize a rescue party. It was him who started walking in spite of his injuries. He had to cover many kilometres in a never-ending snowfall before he reached the lonely police station on the KKH.

The two on-duty officers couldn't believe their eyes and ears when they saw an unsteady white figure emerging from the raging blizzard and heard him call out. They thought that it was probably a ghost. Hazil says they were so shocked that they first tried to keep him at a distance. Then they hurried to make a pot of hot water for him. When he sipped it, he spitted blood again.

Luckily, before long, a bus came skidding down from Khunjerab Pass, occupied by Chinese and Punjabi passengers. He boarded it while dripping water and blood, with chattering teeth, and in a half-dead state. Nobody offered him a seat. They arrived at Sost, a place with Ismaili Volunteers, just like Shimshal. It was the volunteers to whom Hazil now reported the tragedy. The following day, some eight jeeps set off in the direction of the disaster, loaded with clothes, rescuers, hot tea, chapatis, and some hastily collected warm clothes. Hazil felt terrible but he joined them. It was particularly his chest that burned and ached because he had been hit by the drum.

The Ismaili Volunteers picked up the group and took them to Sost, where they spent a night. All Shimshalis, except Hazil Shah, who was at the end of his tether, then embarked on the cheerless journey home.

In Dut, which is a green oasis planted with poplars and

willows, about 18 km from the starting point of the link road to Shimshal, they dug up the graves for the two deceased and paid their last respects to them.

Hazil Shah, who had gone to Aliabad by bus, was in a condition which the local doctors refused to treat. They sent him to a hospital in Gilgit. It was ascertained that he had spat out most of the blood from his internal injuries; otherwise he would not have survived. He got various kinds of medicine but it took him quite some time to recover. The pain in his chest did not fully vanish until three years later.

East of Shimshal is a massive landmark of a mountain, which Hazil calls his 'favourite peak'. This is because at one point in his life he got the idea of organizing the first-ever climb on it, a dream which indeed came true. In 2002, he arranged a sponsorship from an army general so that the operation could be successfully performed. He assembled thirteen Shimshalis, including eminent climbers such as Rajab Shah, Mohammad Ullah, and Yousaf Khan. According to Hazil, he was the group leader, though I will learn a different version of the story in my interview with Yousaf Khan.

The mountain, which had so far been nameless, turned out to be a difficult climb. Its glacier was riddled with crevasses which were hard to negotiate; some passages were being hit by frequent rock-falls; the last ascent was extremely steep and required many lengths of rope. In the end, they had to forgo the real summit. It was impossible for them to climb. They had to be content with a secondary summit, which according to Hazil, is 6,354 metres high.

After the expedition, the members insisted on calling the mountain 'Hazil Peak'. He rejected the idea. Hazil suggested calling it *Yir Khatak*, which means sunrise peak in Wakhi. His modesty was appreciated and the mountain has since been called Sunrise Peak.

Starting in 2003, there is some confusion in Hazil's memories, which can also be noticed on his CV printed at the back of his business card.

One interesting story about Hazil's experiences as a HAP relates to a resounding name, Marcel Kurpershoek, ambassador of the Netherlands to Pakistan. I met him in Shimshal in November 2003, and my diary entries reveal how strong an impression the man made on me. He had strayed into Shimshal because he is a passionate runner, hiker, and trekker. He carried a copybook in which he took notes of Wakhi words such as *chiz-oli, chilpndoc, hresta*. He also had an interest in and sympathy for any sort of dialogue partner.

For Hazil Shah, Marcel Kurpershoek is also 'my good friend'. In 2004, he climbed Mingli Sar with him and thereupon tried Muztagh Ata in China (they did not reach the summit though). In 2005, they went to Spantik together (up to camp 2) and afterwards to the summit of Sonia Peak. Hazil says that he was even invited to the ambassador's Islamabad residence at a time when Kurpershoek was the Dean of all the ambassadors and a 'good friend' of General Musharraf too.

Between 2008 and 2012, Hazil joined trekkers around Shimshal. Among other things, he crossed Orjol Dur Pass from Virjerav Glacier.

Several times during the interview, a tapestry announcing 'My Dream K-2' caught my attention. I cannot refrain from asking Hazil about this dream. He confirms that he considers himself able to climb the 'King of Mountains' if he finds a team and 'a chance', which means money. However, here I would like to quote him literally, describing the big obstacles on his way to K-2. He says, 'My wife is big problem. She said you will not climb more because you are very alone up there. That's big problem for us. Our children is study. You can only going for small peaks like Sonia, like Mingli Sar. This is special request for you. You can stop eight thousand; only six thousand I can give you permission. Very hard for me.'

At this, I ask him point-blank that if ATP hired him for K-2, would he go?

He says that he wants to as he shares this dream with his sister, and also because his sister made such a beautiful tapestry projecting his dream on it. He says that his heart is torn between fulfilling his own wish to climb K-2 and the obligations that come along with having one's own family.

In the end, I want to know what he expects of the younger generation. 'They should accomplish something that advances and promotes Shimshal, like my tourist lodge,' he says. He asks if he could advertise his tourist lodge in this book. He sees himself as an unflagging workman, who, in turn, can proudly present the fruits of his hard work.

Indeed, a few days prior to the interview he had just arrived with his wife from the high pastures, along with his yaks, and with a huge pack on his back, when three visitors from Germany arrived at his tourist lodge, expecting to be accommodated and fed by Hazil Shah.

That is when he feels his element.

Notes

1. Ziarat is the shrine of Saint Hazrat Shamas near Shimshal.
2. Northern Areas Transport Corporation.
3. See in Meherban Shah and Aziz Baig's chapters.
4. Hans Kammerlander, born 1956 in Italy, is one of the world's most prominent high-altitude climbers and particularly famous for his ski expedition on Mt. Everest in 1996.

2.7

Amruddin

High-altitude porter, born 1965

AMRUDDIN IS VISIBLY SURPRISED WHEN WE TURN UP FOR THE interview. He is of a smaller and sturdier build than many others, and I am astonished at how heavy his breathing sounds. However, according to Samad this is common in his family.

Amruddin is a typical example of what I earlier called Shimshal's natural talent. He started with minimal climbing instruction (not counting his three climbs of Mingli Sar) on Nanga Parbat, and indeed reached the summit.

He is a lively, frank, and amiable character, who readily explains possibly bothersome and repeated questions, and answers them jovially. Despite his relatively short career he has a lot to tell. His daughter Bano, 17 years of age, is a member of the SMS girls' team. Some expert observers say she is one of the few whose skills meet higher standards.

Amruddin went to school for a mere three years and does not speak English. The rest of his youth was spent in a totally different occupation. For almost twelve years, he worked as a winter shepherd living far from Shimshal in the Pamir to tend to the yaks. This means that you bid farewell in October and don't come back until mid-May of next year. The winter shepherds are surrounded by snow and ice for seven months and dwell in a rough hut, which only marginally protects them from the winds and the cold.

I make him describe this daily life in extreme conditions in more detail. In the morning, after you have milked the yaks, you open the *vandan*,[1] and let the animals out. They dig through the deep snow until they reach the withered grass grown during the summer by irrigating it through an artful but tedious system. When they have finished it up after some weeks, you move on to the next pasture, in a traditional pattern, for the fodder is bound to suffice for seven months. Like in summer, you make butter and cheese, only less of it, and mainly for your own consumption; or for visitors, for occasionally, if the snow conditions permit, relatives struggle across the Pass in order to supplement the shepherds' stocks with flour, tea, sugar et cetera.

Amruddin's climbing career was short and intense. One day, he took a peek into one of the training sessions that Rajab Shah and Meherban Shah staged on Malangutti Glacier, and was hooked. He approached Qudrat Ali, who had already made his name as a high-altitude porter. He wondered if Qudrat could arrange a job for him too. Qudrat had been hired for Nanga Parbat by the German Ralf Dujmovits in September 2001, and he agreed to take Amruddin along with him. When I ask him incredulously whether Nanga Parbat really was his first 'serious' mountain, he replies in the negative and tells me that it was Mingli, which he climbed thrice with trekkers and also opened a new route. Obviously he considered these three successful climbs insignificant and didn't wish to boast about them.

There were fifteen Germans in Ralf's team. Amruddin depicts the Diamir Face between camp 1 and camp 2 as particularly dangerous. It was mainly bare rock with little or loose snow cover. At one point, they had just fixed a few lengths of rope when an avalanche swept it away into the void. Although Amruddin says he had to carry up to twenty-five kg, he praises the expedition leader Dujmovits and the way he was dealing with both the members and the high-altitude porters. The latter were asked to join the group to the summit because they were to help break the trail, which is the most arduous part on an expedition. In this way, a most remarkable success was attained: eight participants, among them two women, made it to the summit of Nanga Parbat without supplementary oxygen.

With eighteen climbers from various countries (and a Dutch expedition leader), Amruddin was on Broad Peak in 2002. The other HAPs were Balti and Amruddin was the only Shimshali. The group managed to climb as far as camp 3 but some of the members were not in good condition. They suffered from the usual problems: headaches, trouble with the stomach and, of course, high-altitude sickness. Additionally, the weather turned bad and completely thwarted any summit bid. On the descent, it was the HAPs' job to take care of the sick ones, to lend them a hand, support them, and encourage them. It was quite a pitiable lot that finally arrived in the safety of base camp.

In the summer of 2003, Amruddin was busy with construction work on his property in Shimshal; the high-altitude portering had to pause.

Once again with the Baltis, he joined a 16-member international expedition to K-2 in 2004. I want to know how he perceives his cooperation with Baltis. Are they friends, or is there a sense of competition and rivalry? Without hesitation he says that it's a good relationship, but he then starts to ponder as well. Occasionally he has found them to be a little unreliable. He says it did happen that they faked some problem or illness in an attempt to be spared from the summit bid. The payment, according to Amruddin, is the same, independent of the summit bid. Those who are cool and calculating prefer to avoid the hazards of the last stage.

The expedition leader and the members on K-2 this summer handled the issue of the porters' loads in a liberal fashion. Amruddin says he carried between twelve and fifteen kg. However, the summit of K-2 remained out of reach for the whole group. Due to the onset of unfavourable weather, the Bottleneck was the terminus of the expedition even after two months of climbing. At this point, I cannot help adding that it is anyhow a great achievement to have climbed K-2 up to the Bottleneck.

The very same year the 'King of Mountains' was again in Amruddin's programme. It was to be his last expedition. There were too many traumatic experiences that it had had in store for him. Too clearly did he realize how thin the thread is by which a climber's life hangs.

It was a joint expedition of the Pakistani and Chinese Alpine Clubs. Eight Chinese and three Pakistanis participated, among them Captain Iqbal of Pakistan Army, who was already mentioned in Meherban Shah's chapter. The expedition was scheduled for two months. With Amruddin was another Shimshali high-altitude porter, Farzar Khan.

With Farzar, he had been on the way to camp 2, when a huge avalanche swept down. Their lives were saved by two favourable circumstances. First, they were clipped to fixed ropes, which gave them a better foothold and more safety. Second, their position was below an almost vertical passage so the masses of snow did not rip them off or bury them but swept past over them. Nevertheless, the horror of this incident has been deeply engraved on Amruddin's mind. He describes the storm which the avalanche had triggered, and the powder-like snow that he was unable to keep out of his nose and mouth. Such was the violence of the elements that he had to stop breathing.

A short time later, Amruddin was ordered to climb above camp 2 and replace a rope which had been torn by a rock-fall. While he was working there in the precipitous rocks, he happened to be inadvertently careless for the fraction of a second (in this exposed spot, it could have meant death), and slipped on an ice slab. He did stop his fall with great presence of mind but thudded on the rock so hard that he heard a crack: two of his ribs were broken!

He tried to ignore the pain. He would have to tolerate it for another four weeks was what he reckoned, but wrongly so.

What happened was a turn in the weather. Amruddin was by Captain Iqbal's side when they encountered the Chinese and two of the Pakistani members who were descending. They had decided to discontinue the expedition. They said that it was hopeless to keep going in such weather conditions. However, Captain Iqbal did not wish to give up. It would be contrary to his attitude and his skills. He asked Amruddin to continue.

They had to let the descending party pass them. This meant moving to a different rope. As usual, several fixed ropes were running there, some of them from earlier years. Captain Iqbal, who was a seasoned climber, chose one that was a bit further away from him. To catch it he had to jump. Whether the impact of his weight tore the rope from its anchor, or the rope had been brittle in the first place, or it was cut by the sharp edge of a rock, Captain Iqbal fell. Right in front of Amruddin and the others, he fell an almost vertical 600 metres and came to a halt near advanced base camp.

No one had the time to process the shock. Amruddin, deeply shattered for the third time already on this expedition, helped salvage Captain Iqbal's dead body and carry it to base camp. There, he was by no means in a position to relax, for he had to walk at least seventy kilometres with his broken ribs. He says he spent twenty days in hospital in Skardu, showing how seriously he was injured. He covered his expenses from his HAP salary and tips. Either he had not been insured by the Alpine Club, or he had not been informed about a possible refund. Amruddin shrugs his shoulders stoically and says, after all no lasting damage has been done.

What lasted, however, was his determination to turn his back on high-portering.

When asked what advice he would give to today's younger generation, Amruddin, too, ranks education at the top, although he has not followed his own creed. His daughter Bano left school early. He approved of her membership in the SMS girls' team, which means she was in the elite group on their first few expeditions. Unfortunately, it also means that she does not speak English and will probably live a traditional life in Shimshal, interspersed perhaps by the occasional girls' expedition, which according to Ali Musa is 'just for excitement'.

I, however, do not see a problem with that. The village needs the likes of Bano just as it needs highly educated young people who have no leaning towards climbing. If Shimshal wants to succeed in walking the thin line between tradition, progress, and loss, it cannot do without a Bano.

Note

1. The yaks' yard.

2.8

Aziz Baig

High-altitude porter, born 1960

WHEN AZIZ BAIG GREETS US, HE APPEARS AMIABLE BUT also reserved, quiet, and sparing of gestures and facial expressions. He is tall and slim and looks quite young for his age. Samad has whispered to me that he considers him 'very strong'.

While talking, Aziz does not make a fuss of himself either. His voice is gentle and his speech thoughtful. However, you will soon understand why there are so many smile wrinkles around his eyes. His manifold stories—the dramatic as well as the bizarre and obscure ones, and the smart as well as the annoying ones—create smiles.

Like most of my interviewees, Aziz does not take us to the family room where every-day life is going on, but to a newly built edifice nearby. A lot of Shimshalis, including almost all HAPs, have been able to afford building these new places in the past few years. Even though its dimensions are ample and the carpeting and cushions shiny new, and the wooden pillars present themselves in white freshness as opposed to the soot-blackened ones in the old house, the room is not homely. Its sheer size and emptiness and, of course, the lack of a fireplace, make it seem cold. High up, nailed to the roof beam inconspicuously, I see a few photos of Aziz Baig in the obligatory summit pose.

His list of expeditions is impressive. Since 1996, he has had a high-porter job every year, always on eight-thousand-metre peaks, except in 1996 and 2004.

Aziz was orphaned at the age of 16 and attended school for five years. This is all I learn about his childhood. If my interviewees do not go into details unsolicited, I do not insist. He does not remember the precise year of leaving Shimshal; instead, he remembers the purpose. There were several 20-litre canisters of kerosene to be carried to Shimshal, and he helped to haul them.

The idea of climbing was planted in his head by Rajab Shah, who, along with Shambi Khan, was excelling through expeditions and explorations around Shimshal. This was what Aziz also wanted to try. So he participated in one of Rajab's training sessions on Malangutti. On his first expedition, he promptly reached the summit of a quite difficult seven-thousand-metre peak. This was the 1996 tour to Passu Peak (7,478 metres) that has been mentioned twice on previous pages. Aziz was one of those who had to pull Hazil Shah from out of two 30-metre-deep crevasses.

He says that this gave him doubts and he thought more about the kind of path he had taken. He asked himself if he really wanted to take such risks, or possess the mental strength that is required. These questions became even more pressing during his first night on camp 1. He says that he suffered a real crisis, for he had a raging headache. Sleep was unimaginable; he kept tossing and turning in his tent all night and had but a single thought: Back home to Shimshal and never start again!

When he felt better the next morning, the clouds of doubt had vanished. He thought that the idea of quitting was nonsensical, and so he continued. Afterwards, standing on the summit among the other Shimshalis, he was finally imbued with the spirit of climbing.

The very next year, he celebrated his biggest achievement. As mentioned in Mohammad Ullah's chapter, he took part in the joint Pakistani-Chinese expedition on Nanga Parbat. Of the four Shimshalis (Rajab Shah, Yousaf Baig, Tafat Shah, Aziz Baig), two—Aziz and Mohammad Ullah—reached the summit, along with six Tibetans. I ask Aziz about the dangers of rock-falls and avalanches that usually plague Nanga Parbat. He says they were lucky to climb relatively undisturbed. Still, the tour was not without its usual drama. He can relate a smaller incident and a massive one that kept him on tenterhooks for many scary hours. Both happened on the summit bid and during the following night.

In accordance with the custom, they had started at night time and made good progress. At sunrise, the summit seemed to have clearly moved closer. When the sun had risen completely, he wanted to put on his sunglasses. He reached into the top compartment of his back pack where they were supposed to be, and was appalled to notice that he had left them in the tent. He instantly knew that he would have to turn back, otherwise he would inevitably become snow-blind. It was unwise to take such a risk. At his fastest possible pace, he descended to camp 4, and then climbed back up again.

Of course, the others had long since arrived at the summit, waved flags, and taken photos. Something was wrong with Mohammad Ullah though. They did not need to tell him that; he immediately noticed. Without delay, he prompted Mohammad Ullah to join him on the descent. He did not turn to look at him but concentrated on his own safety. Suddenly, he heard Mohammad shout his name.

Aziz thought that maybe he was in need of water. He took out his bottle from the backpack and lodged it visibly near the route, but he did not wait. Briefly afterwards, Aziz heard him shout in desperation, 'Aziz, you must wait for me!' Many minutes passed until Mohammad caught up with Aziz.

'What's the matter? Did you drink enough water?' Aziz inquired.

'Aziz, I am falling asleep. I can't help it; I feel I will collapse.' Mohammad replied.

Aziz now talked seriously and tried to make him drink a substantial amount of water. Mohammad sat on his back pack, took a sip, tilted over, and was asleep! Aziz, himself on the edge of total exhaustion, tried to shake him awake. It took him several attempts. In the end he managed—with Mohammad always on his arm or close before him—infinitely slowly, to descend to camp 4. To his dismay, he found out that the others had already gone. Obviously, they wanted to reach camp 3 on the same day. He was alone with the apathetic, no longer responsive Mohammad Ullah.

What followed was the worst night Aziz had ever lived through. It had soon become clear to him that Mohammad should definitely not be allowed to sleep for then he would stop breathing. Once or twice, he gasped for air like someone choking and then became silent. Aziz poked him, shook him, shouted in his ear, brought him back to life, and the game started over again. This meant that Aziz himself could not sleep because he had to watch over Mohammad so he did not drift off. Every ten minutes, he had to repeat the routine of jolting, shouting, and slapping, so that his comrade did not die under his very eyes. Aziz says he incessantly prayed to God for dawn, his own life, and his friend's survival.[1]

The following day seems to deserve only few words. The condition of someone who suffers from high-altitude sickness—and that is what had happened to Mohammad—improves with every metre of descent. Aziz says that when they reached camp 2, Mohammad had visibly recovered. The rest of the group, however, had definitely vanished. They had descended to base camp on this day.

Aziz experienced something else with his charge. The following scene happened on the last stage: when they were standing above the Diamir Face, where ropes were fixed. Aziz prompted his friend to go first, but Mohammad refused as he was not fully well yet. Aziz clipped his harness to the rope and started to concentrate on the difficult passage when suddenly he heard Mohammad say, 'Aziz, stop there and take a photo of me as I climb.' Aziz hesitated as it was not safe to linger in a vertical face and simultaneously fumble with a camera.

'Come on. I will take one of you too, later,' said Mohammad. Aziz gnashed his teeth, searched for a reasonably safe position, and pressed the button. He then climbed back up three or four metres, held the camera out to Mohammad, and said, 'Now you take one of me. I also want one from this perspective.' At this point, Mohammad had changed his mind and refused. He did not even reach for the camera. He said he was afraid to descend first.

Today Aziz laughs about it but at that moment, he had become awfully angry and was close to hurling the camera into the abyss. He did think of something better though. He turned in silence, left Mohammad on the spot, and got away without a single look back.

In 1998, Aziz Baig had a job in one of the above-mentioned major Japanese expeditions on Gasherbrum-II. Unlike Qurban

Mohammad, Rajab Shah, and Meherban Shah, he had to do without the summit.

The following year, Aziz again joined the Japanese climbers; this time to Broad Peak. This expedition could be labelled 'business as usual', had it not been for a very special expedition leader. He was a type that inordinately weighed down the HAPs' spirits, Aziz says.

He kept ordering them around and could not by any means be contented. He also had an obsession that made him an almost legendary, or rather, infamous figure.

He commanded the high-altitude porters to carry full water containers from camp 2 to camp 3. Carry water at this elevation—was he serious? The porters cast furtive glances among themselves. What were they supposed to do? This order was something unheard-of and very foolish. They thought that water would only add to the weight and would arrive at camp 3 in the form of ice blocks. Isn't it a fact that all high-altitude climbers collect snow and melt it on gas burners to make tea or soup? Can anything be more plausible, more obvious? To their misfortune, this Japanese was adamant and wished to save the costly EPI gas.

I forgot to ask Aziz whether they obeyed. They probably did. HAPs are a dependent lot, who have to adjust even to the likes of this man. In the interviews that follow, I will again hear about the 'crazy Japanese leader' from a countryman of his, Ali Musa's friend Kazuya Hiraide.

To Aziz's misfortune, he again came to work under the thumb of this Japanese leader the next summer, this time on K-2. The carrying of water now began from advanced base camp and ended at camp 3. Nothing could dissuade the 'crazy leader' from this idea firmly rooted in his mind. Aziz struggled, but eventually slaved away. He contracted abdominal pain

upon reaching camp 3. The stomach ache and spasms were
so fierce that he had to descend in a hurry and rush to Skardu.
The doctor did not take long to diagnose his problem. It was
dehydration. He urged Aziz in serious words to drink no less
than four litres each day while on tour. This was probably the
best solution as he has not suffered any problems since. By the
way, the rest of the team did not proceed further than camp 3.

    With six Australians, Aziz Baig was on Broad Peak in 2001.
Bad weather at camp 4 thwarted their summit bid, but there
is one episode from this expedition which Aziz remembers
vividly. Along with another Shimshali, Wahab Ali Shah, he was
on the ascent and had arrived at camp 2. They were going to
continue after a short break, for it was their task to pitch the
tents of camp 3 further up. On the way, they had heard of
an American woman who had been abandoned by her high-
altitude porter or Sherpa. She was believed to be at camp 2.
The two Shimshalis had been informed about the location of
her tent. They found it closed, lifeless. They could not decide
whether she had gone or was inside, or if she was even well
enough to respond. The two knocked on the tent poles. There
wasn't any response. They knocked once again, but again there
was no answer. Aziz asked Wahab to open the zipper in order
to look inside.

    'No, I won't do this. You do it. I dislike the idea. It is
disrespectful,' Wahab said.

    However, at this very moment, there was something more
important at stake than respect so Aziz opened the tent. They
saw a woman of medium age cocooned in her sleeping bag
up to the tip of her nose. Was she asleep? Aziz had to jolt her
by her shoulder, since she did not react to calling. A pair
of unconscious, oblivious eyes looked at the two men. The
woman did not show any expressions.

'Are you all right?' Aziz asked. She nodded.

Then Aziz said, 'We will go to camp 3 now, but on our way back we will take care of you and help you walk further down.'

It took the friends a good five hours to return to the American's tent. She did not seem to have stirred in all that time. Her position on the mattress was exactly the same as before. The two men overcame their inhibitions, crept into the tent, propped her up, fitted her in her harness, boots, crampons, and put her outside in front of the tent. Aziz says she swayed helplessly and could not take a single step without support. It was now the Shimshalis' job to escort the woman down in one way or another—a difficult task and one that required patience.

Anyhow, she gradually gained consciousness and could eventually walk more safely. She seemed to be aware of her condition and good fortune, and began to express her relief and gratitude towards Wahab and Aziz. The closer they got to the base camp, the more wonderfully she adorned the praise of her two saviours and their phenomenal commitment. They finally arrived at the base camp around 9 p.m., where the woman promised them queenly rewards.

'I will do many things for you,' Aziz still remembers the woman's words. To confirm her pledges, she warmly hugged them.

'And then nothing happened,' Aziz says in disappointment.

With a group of six Poles and minus the summit, Broad Peak was Aziz Baig's workplace in 2003 too.

In 2004, it was K-2 again. He was with an international team of strong climbers. However, due to bad weather the Bottleneck had to be their terminus.

With two Balti HAPs, Aziz was hired by four Japanese women on the seven-thousand-metre peak, Muztagh Ata, in

2005. The ladies were believed to be seasoned climbers, for they had been on top of Mount Everest. When they expressed their wish to skip camp 3 and combine the last two stages from camp 2 (at 6,200 metres) to the summit, the high-altitude porters did not object. They did not put it past them to have the stamina and expertise to cover a technically easy 1,300 metres in one go. Despite these prerequisites, 1,300 metres high up 'in thin air', where you have to expend a lot more energy than in the Alps for instance, remain a challenge. Circumstances transpired exactly as expected. One of the ladies began to totter above camp 3. She complained of a pain in her chest, ice-cold feet, and headache. Although the group halted every few steps to catch their breath, she claimed she could not recover her strength. She seriously delayed the climb.

Aziz resorted to a trick. As described in Farhad Khan's chapter, as you move closer to Muztagh Ata's summit the terrain gets flatter, but climbing it becomes a grim and endless slog. On that day visibility was close to zero. Aziz accelerated his step, advanced some fifty metres, raised his arms, and announced, 'We have arrived at the summit, only a few more metres to cover!' When they caught up with him, happy and gasping, he said, 'Well, maybe just another five minutes! We will easily manage.' He turned his back to them and did the same again. He does not remember how often he repeated it. Eventually the trick succeeded and all climbers reached the summit, but they got too late. Now they faced a descend in complete darkness with the little light of headlamps. At this point, the ladies suddenly remembered that they hadn't even packed their headlamps. Filled with consternation, rummaging through their backpacks several times, pleading, and whimpering, each one asked the other if she had found her headlamp. Even the high-altitude porters hadn't carried their lamps.

They now faced a dilemma as to what to do in such a situation. One of the Baltis, who was most familiar with the route, was willing to hurry down to camp 3 and beg a strong torch of its residents. He planned to use it to send up light signals and, if necessary, climb back to help the clients descend safely.

Somehow, everybody ended up undamaged. In spite of the fog, the little bunch of climbers managed to grope their way into the second camp and, long after midnight, collapsed on their mattresses.

In the summer of 2005, Aziz Baig worked on K-2 for a twelve-member international team, two of whom made it to camp 4.

With seven Frenchmen in 2006, Gasherbrum-II was his next destination. They remained on the mountain for a month, restrained by heavy snowfall from climbing beyond camp 1.

Aziz's 2007 expedition to Broad Peak with four Japanese climbers also ended prematurely. One female member suddenly developed the symptoms of high-altitude sickness in camp 3. The HAPs had to take her down speedily. This was done well between camps 3 and 2 by holding, propping, and guiding her, Aziz says. From camp 2, however, he and a Balti had to take turns in carrying her to the base camp. She was picked up by a helicopter and taken to Skardu, but what happened to her after that is not known to Aziz.

In 2008, the year of disaster, he was also on K-2 but considerably earlier than his fellow Shimshalis, Jehan Baig and Meherban Karim. He made it to camp 4 with nine Japanese but had to turn back due to too much new snow. Only after returning to the village did he learn of the two Shimshalis' deaths.

I wonder whether Aziz Baig finds differences among national characters, whether there are certain typical traits that distinguish, say, the Japanese from the French or the British. Without hesitation, he speaks of the Germans and compliments them. According to him, they are always strong mountaineers. Mostly, their conduct is friendly and conciliatory except for when they are 'emotional' (which for Shimshalis can be a synonym for 'angry'). In such cases, he says, Germans are hard to deal with but what's appreciable about them is that they mostly break their own trails and go to their very limits on the summit bid. Others have the HAPs make the route, which he calls 'lazy'.

Another attempt at climbing Broad Peak in 2009 with three Poles ended without a summit bid, just as in 2003.

In 2010 and 2011, Aziz Baig was with Farhad Khan on the international double expeditions on Broad Peak and K-2. Other than Farhad, he recalls more than the ordinary facts and shares grim details of an unfortunate and distressing episode on Broad Peak in 2011.

Among those who had made it to the highest camp and were now preparing for the summit bid, there was a Chinese climber. This man's condition had deteriorated a lot during the night. He was vomiting and had shown clear indications of high-altitude sickness. The mountain guide refused to include him in the summit bid. Beyond all reason, the Chinese would not cooperate. Coughing and wobbling, at 2:30 a.m., he joined the group of those who started for the summit. With an incredible display of willpower, he reached the 'V'—a crucial point not far from the summit of Broad Peak which looks like the letter V. Sadly, all his stubbornness could not help him as he had to turn back from here. He could certainly not be left alone. The leader instructed a HAP to join him. The HAP was supposed to guide him on the descent and, if necessary, hold him by his harness.

Yet, once again the Chinese man's obstinacy got the better of him. He shouted, stamped his feet, and struggled.

'What shall I do? He does not listen. I can't even go near him,' the guide asked the expedition leader.

The leader asked him to at least try to help the Chinese safely cross one particular crevasse. Then, in God's name, he could let him go.

Nothing came of it. The man balked. He rejected any kind of assistance. The guide eventually gave up and frankly, what else could he have done? He was being threatened, at almost eight thousand metres. There is a limit to helpfulness.

The Chinese tried to jump and slipped. He tumbled and fell into the crevasse. He must have died in a matter of seconds. The team had to leave him right there. Retrieving a dead body at that altitude is impossible.

In the summer of 2012, Aziz Baig was on the snow-laden tour to Gasherbrum-II with Sarwar Ali. He narrates the lengthy and futile attacks on the mountain. At the leader's command, Aziz had to try blazing a trail above camp 2. He shakes his head and says that he was completely hopeless about it. When the snow is shoulder-high, you have to throw in the towel. The leader tried it too and instantly acknowledged that moving forward was by no means possible. He positioned himself in front of the members and announced that, unfortunately, it was now the end of the expedition. One of them was a Swiss national and he protested. He refused to believe that camp 2 was already the terminus. 'I want to check personally. I need to know the truth,' he said. He ended up getting caught in the same useless struggle as the two before him. They had given their best and were entitled to retreat with their heads held high. Failure was due to external circumstances, not to a lack of climbing skills.

When I ask Aziz Baig about the HAPs' wages, he speaks of one-thousand rupees per day. Compared to the Sherpas' payments, it is little. They get an extra five-hundred dollar bonus when they make it to camp 4. He suspects that a lot of the money which Western climbers pay to the tour operators disappears into their pockets.

We have come to the end of the interview. Aziz reckons he will add two or three more years to his high-portering job. He is aware of his age and accepts his limits, but since his job is also what finances his children's education, he wants to make use of his potential.

Note

1. The so-called sleep or high-altitude apnoea strikes many climbers at high altitudes but is not dangerous to life, as Aziz feared.

2.9

Amin Ullah Baig

High-altitude porter, born 1972

AMIN ULLAH BAIG GREETS US WITH A BIG SMILE. HE IS wearing Gore-Tex and a baseball cap, and seems to look forward to being interviewed. He also takes us to a newly built house where I feel a bit like a mouse forlorn in an arena. However, this feeling passes at once because Amin irresistibly draws me into the spell of his stories. During the first half of the interview, Samad is translating but it turns out that Amin knows enough English to describe his career to me himself. This career is rich with details. Through his openness, Amin reveals his personality, his character as a human being, and his strengths and weaknesses.

His 2012 experience of being in the middle of an avalanche exceeds everything else, also because he has a very special way of talking about it.

Amin Ullah Baig attended the Government School for Boys in Shimshal for eight years and thus is one of the countless male students who were taught by the esteemed Daulat Amin. Right after school, Amin turned to 'tourism', which means that he joined trekking and mountaineering groups in the region of his village. Being the only son, he was obliged even at the tender age of fifteen to financially support his two sisters.

His first tour with four Koreans took him from Passu to Lupgar Sar (7,200 metres). The weather was bad but the payment was good, he says. At that time, it was a really nice compensation for a hard-working fifteen-year-old boy.

During the 1990s, he mostly joined trekking groups. Not only did he carry loads for them, but also chopped vegetables and washed dishes as an assistant cook. On these tours, he had the opportunity to climb Mingli Sar twice. One of the expeditions was with a group of Oxford students, who planted an idea in him: why not try high-attitude climbing? He decided to participate in one of Rajab Shah's training sessions on the Malangutti Glacier. However, a few years were to pass before he could put his skills into practice.

In 1999, he got lucky. For some reason he had gone to Passu, where he met a Frenchman who had just climbed Muztagh Ata in China. They started to talk. The Frenchman said that he was staying for ten more days— would Amin like to join him to Shimshal Pass? Up there, he learned that this climber was planning an expedition to Gasherbrum-II the following year. He offered Amin a job as a HAP and promised to contact him by any means. He also asked Amin to bring along two of his strong Shimshali friends.

He kept his promise. The message came in the spring of 2000 and Amin took his friends Sajjad Karim and Wahab Ali Shah with him to Gasherbrum-II. For the three of them, it was their first eight-thousand-metre peak, and all reached the summit straight away. Amin laughs and says, 'but the French food was something really strange for the Shimshalis!'

It was two different experiences on this particular expedition which must have had quite an impact on a climbing novice.

One of the members had got inflicted with high-altitude-sickness at camp 1. He had to be taken back to the base camp in a hurry. As usual, it was expected that his condition would improve automatically at a lower altitude. It did not.

On the contrary, he started to hallucinate and then lost consciousness. The expedition leader said that the man's life was in danger. Yet, what was needed without delay—a rescue helicopter with an emergency doctor on board—could by no means be arranged at the base camp of Gasherbrum-II.

The French then dragged something in (which looked like a rubber sack with a zipper and a see-through window), put the sick man inside and, pulled the zipper shut. Amin was appalled to see this. The man was sure to die within minutes.

One of them then started to pump air into the sack so it rose and swelled. Amin learned that it was not air but oxygen, and this was supposed to bring the man back to life.

The three Shimshalis strained their eyes to look through the window and watch the victim's face. All of a sudden the man opened his eyes and even grinned at them. He was evidently being revived and it was unbelievable. After less than an hour he asked to be freed, and jumped and hugged the speechless Shimshalis. That moment onwards, he was the strongest of the bunch.

The other experience left the three beginners in deep shock. During their ascent, not far from the summit of Gasherbrum-II, they met two brothers from Spain who were coming down from the top in a spirit of euphoria, waving and cheering, and looking absolutely happy. Later, when Amin's team was descending, they learned that one of the brothers had fallen to his death due to a torn rope. They knew that they would pass through the place where he fell. They were not spared the gruesome sight of the man's remains, his ripped backpack, and scattered clothes, for the dead body had to be left where it was because of a risk of avalanches.

Climbing is not a child's game. That it could end in death was engraved in the three young men's minds.

After Amin Ullah Baig had paused in 2001, he was again hired by the same Frenchman in 2002. Once again, he was joined by Wahab Ali Shah and Sajjad Karim. This time it was a double expedition to Gasherbrum-I and II with a group of French and Swiss climbers. The boss did not turn up personally; he had sent a different expedition leader.

The two Gasherbrums share the same base camp and camp 1. When Amin mentions the number of expeditions that were milling around in those two camps in 2002, I once again realize the dimensions which high-altitude climbing— particularly its commercial branch—has adopted on the eight-thousand metre peaks. Amin tells me that thirty-five expedition teams were elbowing each other in these places. It almost looked like a tent city whose residents, by their sheer number, were an anonymous crowd, strangers to each other, but all of them moving on the identical narrow and precarious route in the bottlenecks where the masses queue up, and impatience breaks through and tends to spur steps that are fatal. Amin describes a day of clear weather when he could see the route to camp 1 and counted no fewer than seventy-two climbers in a line. They hardly looked more animated than lifeless beads on a string.

When Amin and his two friends were in camp 1, the leader announced that he would climb to camp 2 with one of the participants and spend the night there for acclimatization. The Shimshalis were instructed to ascend to camp 3 the following day and erect tents there. However, this was not to happen as they were later asked to retrieve a dead body instead.

One of the Frenchmen had become high-altitude-sick at camp 2, so early the next morning both of them set off on a hurried descent. Equally early, as the favourable weather had to be exploited, dozens of climbers had started from camp 1 and were obstructing the bottlenecks for those coming down. In order to let one of the ascending people pass on the fixed rope, one of the Frenchmen unclipped his karabiner, lost his foothold, and fell to his death. Not much later, the three Shimshalis saw the other one coming towards them.

It seemed that he was close to a breakdown. Sobbing uninhibitedly, he told them of the accident. He kept blaming himself for not preventing it. He was at a loss. How was he to convey the sad news to the family?

This was the second time that Amin had been confronted with death on the mountain. As high-altitude porters, he and his companions were not allowed to succumb to the shock. They had to keep functioning and remain firm and steady as rocks. They descended to the deceased, retrieved his body and some of his belongings that had come loose in the fall, and took everything to camp 1. From there, they were to go back to the base camp and bring a stretcher to camp 1 the same day. Shortly before midnight, while they were pulling the zippers of the tent and their sleeping bags shut, they got a radio call. It said that the helicopter would come the next day and they must instantly set off with the stretcher in order to get the body down by noon. The zippers were undone, boots came on again, and headlamps were strapped to weary foreheads. In the mess tent, they got some hastily warmed-up tea and a bite of chapati. At 1 a.m. they started into the darkness of the night and arrived at camp 1 at 5 a.m. By 8 o'clock in the morning, they had carried the dead body back to the base camp.

It took the expedition members five days to garner the strength to look past what had happened. They then decided to make another attempt at climbing. Wahab stayed on

Gasherbrum-II with two members and indeed reached the summit. Amin and Sajjad tried Gasherbrum-I and had to draw the line at camp 2.

June of 2004 was a month of continuous snowfall. Amin was on Gasherbrum-I with Jehan Baig and had the opportunity to chat with Qudrat Ali, who at that time still worked as a high-altitude porter for ATP, and returned frostbitten. Through this contact, Amin also met with the renowned climbing couple Ralf Dujmovits and Gerlinde Kaltenbrunner. For all climbers on the two Gasherbrums, be it the HAP, expedition member, or leader, the daily occupation was the drudgery of breaking a trail over and over again, which was mainly futile since the wind and new snow soon buried the route again. In spite of the endless work and frustration, Amin and Jehan eventually made it to the summit of Gasherbrum-I along with the Dutch couple, Katja and Henk, who were members of Ralf and Gerlinde's expedition. They became the first Dutch to summit Gasherbrum-I. Incidentally, it was Jehan Baig's first ever attempt on an eight-thousand-metre peak. What was a helpful device, according to Amin, was Ralf's 'weathercast machine', which impressed him a lot. In fact we know from Gerlinde and Ralf how precise the (now retired) Austrian Charly Gabl's forecasts had always been, and how they were decisive for exploiting windows of good weather.

Not unlike two years before, in the 2005 trip the summit of Gasherbrum-II was already within reach for Amin and his Mexican employers. He says that they were only 200 metres away from the highest point. Although the climbers were strong and healthy, they climbed very slowly. Since the weather was likely to deteriorate, the sensible decision was to turn their back on the summit.

In 2006, Amin Ullah Baig was with Sajjad Karim and

a Swiss group on a double expedition to Broad Peak and Gasherbrum-I. When the two of them had established camp 3 on Broad Peak, Sajjad began to complain of kidney pain. The problem rapidly worsened in base camp. At this, Amin sought permission from the expedition leader to escort his friend on the way to Skardu. As has been learned from Hazil Shah, Shimshalis walk the four to five trekking stages between base camp and Payu in less than one day. In Payu, Sajjad's condition was slightly better and he could continue on his own. Amin walked back to the base camp and was told that the expedition on Broad Peak was finished and the group was now turning to Gasherbrum-I. He was completely nonplussed and protested: 'Haven't we already established camp 3? All of it will be in vain! Are you really serious?' He could not dissuade the expedition members. They did not want to miss their chance on Gasherbrum-I. As he wondered what would become of camp 3 on Broad Peak where sleeping bags, down suits, oxygen bottles, and other precious equipment had been deposited, the expedition members decided that it would be collected after the Gasherbrum-I climb.

Unfortunately, neither did they reach the summit of Gasherbrum-I, nor succeeded in saving a single thing from the camp on Broad Peak. In spite of a prolonged search, nothing could be recovered. The things had partly been swept off the mountain by the winds. Partly, they had been buried by giant banks of snow.

With four Portuguese climbers and one Frenchman, Amin Ullah Baig worked on K-2 in 2007. He proudly reveals that one of the climbers was Joao Garcia, a man who was then short of only four of the fourteen eight-thousanders: K2, Broad Peak, Nanga Parbat and Annapurna. K-2 was to be his eleventh eight-thousand-metre peak this summer. Amin thought that if everything went according to this man's plans, some years from now he would be the first Portuguese to have scaled all eight-thousand-metre peaks.

However, new snow had accumulated once again. The climbers struggled for days and weeks through the bottomless masses of snow and finally managed to dig and claw their way to higher altitudes. Amin's group started to cooperate with two Americans and took turns with them breaking the trail. This way, Joao and Amin managed to reach camp 4, which meant that there was only one stage left to make it to the highest point at 8,611 metres.

As a climber, Amin had cherished the bold dream of ascending to K-2's summit for quite some years. God knows what made the very same day seem apt enough to make it come true.

Halfway towards the summit, Amin had to let go of the idea of reaching to the top because he had lost all energy. The tough climb to camp 4 had drained him of his strength.

'I felt I could not summit K-2.' He frankly admits his exhaustion.

He told Joao to go ahead while he would wait for them at camp 4. That day, other climbers and Joao must have stood on the top of K-2. Amin says that the other expeditions heading towards the summit that day included Italians, Russians, and Koreans. One Italian who did not make it until 6 p.m. had disappeared without a trace, and a Sherpa who fell in the Bottleneck remained missing too. Joao, however, had bagged his eleventh eight-thousand-metre peak.

In 2008, Amin had planned to scale Gasherbrum-II but like his fellow Shimshali Sarwar Ali, he was denied the success along with his one French and two Mexican clients.

The following year, Amin Ullah Baig first experienced the folly of a winter expedition.

For decades, there have been winter expeditions, particularly on eight-thousand-metre peaks. I am yet to understand what attracts climbers to them. The protagonists of these winter dramas struggle with the agony of coughing spasms and whimper from cold, with their faces distorted by pain. It must be a very unpleasant experience.

A winter expedition generally lasts for about three months and above. Mess tents and kitchen tents are nowadays insulated by triple outer layers so there is at least one place to sit (in your down suit, of course) without shivering from cold. It's still very tough.

Seventy days was the initially allotted time in winter 2008–09 for an expedition to Broad Peak that was run by two Poles and one Canadian. They had hired Qudrat Ali, Amin Ullah Baig, and two HAPs from Skardu.

'It was too cold and windy up there at the base camp,' Amin laughs while recalling the experience.

The HAPs and expedition members still managed to climb up to 7,200 metres and established camp 3. That was the end. Amin says the estimated wind speed was 100 km/h. Had they tried to approach the summit, they would have simply been swept off the mountain.

What follows now is something that evidently fills Amin with satisfaction. It's about his successful expedition on Nanga Parbat in the summer of 2009, once again with Joao Garcia. He speaks of the element of 'luck' in making this trip successful. He says that climbing becomes easier when there is much snow on Nanga Parbat. This is in total contrast to other mountains where a lot of snow is a hindrance to climbers. On the 'Naked Mountain' [1] though, the difficult thing is climbing on bare rock. Therefore, any thicker snow layer in the gullies makes the ascent easier.

Apart from Joao and himself, there was a Korean woman called Miss Unsen (Or Eun-Sun) with two Sherpas in Amin's group. At 1 p.m. they arrived at the summit after having taken turns in blazing the trail. They took their time savouring this moment of elation, captured a lot of photos, took a little rest, and replenished liquids. The group had long been on the descent when they saw quite sizeable a team moving up. 'Too late' was what immediately occurred to Amin. They would be taking a risk if they were planning to reach the summit the same day. Amin's group tried their best to dissuade this other expedition from going any further. They told them that their arrival at the summit would be around 6 or 7 p.m. and then they couldn't possibly descend in the darkness on this mountain as it was too dangerous. Members of the other expedition turned a deaf ear to the suggestions of Amin's group. The Koreans had a female member, Go Mi-Sun, who insisted on their plan to move further up. They took the risk of descending during the night.

How did the day end for Amin? He reports that the two Sherpas and Miss Unsen stayed in camp 4 and Joao, along with one man from Skardu, spent the night in camp 3. When he indicated that he was going to descend to camp 2, in order to spend the night at the lowest possible altitude, they simply called him 'crazy'. Of course, as a Shimshali, he did descend. He again attributes his success to his 'luck'. He refuses to extol his achievement too obtrusively.

Upon his arrival at the base camp the next day, he heard that a Korean woman had suffered an accident. He thought if by any means this was about Miss Unsen. From Joao and the man from Skardu, he got the devastating news of Go

Mi-Sun's death. After a lengthy and exhausting climb, Go Mi-Sun had been deprived of all her vitality and senses when she finally arrived on the summit. Together with two expedition members and one Pakistani HAP, she had spent the night in the open, scarcely below the summit without a tent, liquids, or supplementary oxygen. They managed to survive and continued their descent. However, between camp 3 and camp 2, she collapsed and died. Amin says that he didn't understand where they possibly went wrong because the fall was so deep that she came to a stop directly above camp 1, totally shattered. It was impossible to collect and retrieve her dead body.

The next summer, Amin Ullah Baig worked on K-2 for an Iranian woman by the name of Leila, who had been the first female of her country to summit Nanga Parbat. Their journey was plagued by bad weather for several days and they lost a lot of precious time. They stayed in camp 3 for three days to wait for a window of good weather, which was not to open for them anytime soon. A year later, in 2011, Leila died on K-2.

In 2011, Amin worked as a HAP for a 16-member German expedition on Nanga Parbat. When camp 2 was established and the group began to discuss their next strategy, seven participants threw in the towel and gave up the climb. They had acknowledged their lack of experience. They argued that in order to ascend Nanga Parbat, one should be an older and more seasoned climber. Confirming this view, Amin says, 'For young people it is very hard.'

Those who stayed made two summit bids—both thwarted by unfavourable weather.

Like some of his colleagues, Amin Ullah Baig also credits the Russians with superior climbing potential. He recalls a winter expedition in 2011–12 with the Russians, when they made a summit bid on K-2 with a 15-member team. This expedition was supported by Amin, Farhad Khan, and two other men from Skardu.

Sub-zero temperatures, gale-force winds, and snowfall are the usual ingredients of a winter expedition. Despite all adversities the Russian expedition managed to climb up to 7,300 metres and installed camp 3 there. It was three Russians who had fixed that. The disclosure of one of them becoming high-altitude-sick came up quite late. His two comrades had not become suspicious until, during the descent, he told them in camp 1 that he had decided to spend the night there instead of accompanying them right to the base camp. He did not reveal anything about his deteriorating health.

Shortly afterwards, he sent a radio message to the base camp and called for urgent help. He felt like dying. He didn't say much and the radio went silent really quick. The expedition leader sent all four HAPs and a Russian climber to camp 1. The sick man stopped shortly after he had started to descend, and seemed totally helpless. Doing their utmost, they first took him to advanced base camp, paused there, and managed to arrive at base camp by 10 p.m. Amin remembers that he had become a little better by then. The expedition doctor treated him with oxygen and medicines. As an additional precaution, a helicopter had been requested from Skardu; however, it could not arrive due to bad weather.

'When the weather is bad in winter, the day is really long. We got unlucky as the bad weather continued for five days,' says Amin.

According to Farhad Khan, it was pneumonia that had struck the poor Russian climber. Four days later, at 11 a.m., the sick man died.

At this point in the interview, we are only left with discussing Amin's expedition during 2012. I would like to have Amin speak personally here—just as he spoke onto my cassette recorder—in his original words with no changes whatsoever.

'This year I'm very lucky man. I was at K-2 with the German person Peter[2] and a Swiss guy. We climbed to K-2 and established camp 1. Peter and I reached base camp evening time. When we were on the way—I was down maybe 200 metre—we took some water and again we started. Suddenly we listen a loud noise, but I don't see anything. It was avalanche. (Laughs)'

'The avalanche push me down and at that time I was forget where I am and we[3] fell down. In the middle I think my head is broken. Then again I think I am coming [in] good condition. And I see I am—I was on the snow. And sometimes snow coming cover me and sometimes I was open, and [with] very fast speed I go down. That time I was six-hundred-metre come down. (Pauses)'

'Then I pray every time to God. It's a new life for me. Now I'm talking with you, otherwise six-hundred-metre down with avalanche normally nobody can survive. I was in the last stage. After the avalanche stopped, I stand up. I check my body. How was my body?'

'When I stand up, my leg is good. I was try to [move] my arm up. It was good. Just in my eyes something is coming. It is just water. Just I check like this (wipes his hand over his forehead and eyes) [and I saw] it was blood.'

'I said, no problem, it's no problem. Now I'm good. And I never see my friend Peter. Where is Peter? It's good luck when I was a little bit on the front because the avalanche push me and Peter is safe. Then I see my feet. My feet is twisted! (Laughs)'

'Then I try to make good decision. That time I was just close my eyes and I take my shoes and I turn (makes a jerking gesture) my feet (Laughs) I turn my feet the same direction. That time I feel very pain but I make my feet good straight.'

'Then I try to go to base camp and there is two person, one Nepali and one Russian woman I think. When I was in the avalanche and I stand up, I see somebody is walking from the glacier. I call them, please help me, I was fell down, but that person cannot help me. That's why little bit shock for me. I think it was crazy. I don't know. But in the mountain like this situation you must be help somebody. But they cannot help me. One Pakistani is from Skardu [was] with that person. Three person was there and I call them, please, come on and help me. I was not [in] a good situation. But nobody come help me.'

Then I was [to] try by myself. [It] is one hour to base camp. I try, try, try, try to [reach] near the base camp. [Then I see] my [expedition] member is coming.[4] "Amin, Amin, you are crazy, you walking! Six-hundred metre you came down and you walking," he said.'

'I says I have a good luck. That's why I walking and come to base camp, and there Peter is phone to Skardu for Askari Aviation.[5] But the system is not good, but they are not coming the same time.'

'I wait five days. My foot pain, my face broken, my head is broken, my arm is [broken]. Everything is injured, but not fractured.'

'Then I said to Peter that I worry about my head. I said please Peter, I want to go by walk, by foot, but they said no. "I pay, already I pay Askari Aviation," Peter said.'

'But they says the weather is bad, the weather is bad, the

weather is bad like this. Then I start next day and I says, Peter, no I cannot stay more, I must be go.'

'Then they come with me to Concordia.[6] Peter is very nice person, and I say okay now I am in Concordia. You go, again, back. There is you have one more client, and you [must] climb more. Then we are in Concordia. Peter is go up, but he [is] afraid. He says must be every day you call me and I says no problem; there is a horse coming and I ride horse and go. No problem, you don't worry. Then the same day horse is coming and next day Naiknam[7] is sent [for] me. He is very nice person, you know? Many time he talk with Askari Aviation. Ashraf[8] also talk with Askari Aviation, but they say weather is not good. Then they send a horse. It is very nice. Then horse arrive there and next day I ride on the horse, and after three day I was in Skardu.'

Upon his arrival in Skardu, Amin went to the local hospital, where he was treated as an in-patient for one day and then for five days as an out-patient. Finally he was sent to a hospital in Gilgit for another three days. The tour operator ATP settled the bills.

With a little more rest and relaxation at home, less than four weeks after his avalanche experience, he felt fit enough to join another expedition to Masherbrum Peak (7,821m). During this expedition, the summit bid had to be called off due to bad weather.

By the end of our interview, his next winter expedition has already been agreed upon. It will be at Broad Peak with Poles for the duration of three months—from December 2012 to February 2013.

Later, in March 2013, I browsed on the internet and learned that two of the members had died, and the expedition had been called off. There were lots of photos on the website of the expedition members. However, not a single high-altitude porter had been photographed.

Despite all difficulties, Amin Ullah Baig's view of the job is utterly positive. He definitely wants to continue working as a HAP, and that too for a long time. When I inquire about his future plans, I learn that he also harbours the dream to stand atop K-2.

'K-2 is very beautiful mountain. I like K-2. If any more chance, I want to climb K-2.'

He also remembers his three failed attempts and seems to derive a measure of level-headedness and realism from those experiences.

Notes

1. 'Naked Mountain' is the literal meaning of Nanga Parbat.
2. Peter Guggemos.
3. Shimshalis tend to say 'we' instead of 'I'.
4. The Swiss man.
5. Airline of the Pakistan Army.
6. Concordia Glacier is the place where the Godwin Austen Glacier (coming from K-2) flows into Baltoro Glacier.
7. One of the senior staff at ATP and Ashraf Aman's brother-in-law.
8. Ashraf Aman, founder of ATP.

2.10

Rajab Shah

High-altitude porter, born 1949

RAJAB SHAH IS A MONUMENTAL PERSON. HIS STATELY FIGURE strikes the eye too. Even if you are unaware that he is the first Pakistani to stand on the summits of all five eight-thousand-metre high peaks of his country, you would somehow fathom the man's eminence.

His large face is distinguished by two slanting eyebrows. I am quite sure that no-one else in Shimshal has got such eyebrows.

Similar to Daulat Amin, who must be called the father of education in Shimshal, Rajab Shah is entitled to be considered the father of climbing not only due to his collection of summits, but also because he has conveyed his knowledge and skills to the younger generation on countless occasions.

Another remarkable thing about Rajab Shah relates to him being the first Shimshali to live permanently in Farmanabad. This newly founded settlement—eight kilometres downstream from Shimshal—has become a green oasis just like the older parts of the village in a surprisingly short period.

Rajab Shah is not only Meherban Shah's long-time climbing companion, but there is another specific connection between them based on a similar blow of fate. Two years prior to the death of Meherban Shah's son Ghulam Ali Shah on Sonia

Peak, Rajab's eldest son Aman Khan died on Momil Glacier in 1999. Rajab Shah has six sons and daughters today. One of them, Raheem Uddin, has a job with an NGO in Kazakhstan.

Similar to Meherban Shah, large representations of the five eight-thousand-metre peaks adorn Rajab's new house in Farmanabad. These pictures are supplemented with the 'Crown of Karakorum', a title which he was officially awarded after completing his climbing series with Gasherbrum-II in 1998. On the same occasion, the Alpine Club of Pakistan published a complete list of Rajab Shah's expeditions from 1986 to 1998, which are fifteen in total. Rajab does not even mention his expeditions of 'easier' summits such as Muztagh Ata (twice) or Mingli Sar. He says his recollection has suffered serious deficiencies owing to his son's death. Shortly thereafter, he abandoned climbing but continued working as an instructor for younger Shimshalis.

For his outstanding achievements, the Pakistani government awarded him one of the highest honours, the 'Pride of Performance' medal. It is granted in the fields of science, art, literature, music, sports, and the like. The internationally renowned Sufi musician Ustad Fateh Ali Khan (d. 1997) was awarded the prize too.

Rajab Shah had two brothers and a sister. He attended school for three years, which is not inconsiderable for his time as Daulat Amin's era was still in the distant future. His teacher was the oft-mentioned Ghulam Sultan of Gulmit. Rajab says Urdu was virtually the only subject. Today, he is surprisingly well-versed in English and, in this, clearly surpasses others of his generation.

It was in 1964 that he first left his village. Back then, he was fifteen years old. He joined a group of yaks loaded with farm produce, which was going from Shimshal to Hunza. His

class fellow Yousaf Khan came along too. During the rule of
the Mir of Hunza—who did not abdicate power until 1974—
Shimshalis had to take care of his yaks in their own high
pastures. On a regular basis, the animal products—butter,
cheese, wool (or woollen carpets)—had to be taken to Hunza
as a tribute to their ruler.

Rajab Shah's first expedition in 1986 was not meant to
be a mountain climb. It was a scientific exploration of some
Karakoram glaciers, which was scheduled for three months.
WAPDA, the government's water authority, in cooperation
with two Canadian glaciologists intended to research both the
history of the glaciers and the local water situation. The focus
was also on the Khurdapin Pass (which was then first crossed),
Baraldu Pass (also called Lukpe La), and Hispar La. Rajab
did not only work as a porter but also as an assistant when,
for instance, ice samples were collected with the help of drills.
From these samples the scientists hoped to draw conclusions
on glacial history. Apart from that, the Canadians were skilled
climbers and excellent skiers. For Rajab, they had brought
along snow shoes.

Rajab had his first experience on K-2 in 1987. There is not
much that he relates about the tour. The team was French
with a female leader. They had fixed camp 3 when a rock fall
occurred. One piece hit the woman and crushed the fingers of
one of her hands. The expedition was cancelled there and then.

In the winter of December 1987–February 1988, Rajab
Shah worked as a high-altitude porter in a K-2 expedition of
colossal dimensions along with another Shimshali, the revered
Mohabbat Shah (d. 2011). The thirty expedition members
came from France, Germany, Italy, Great Britain, Poland, and
Japan. They had probably combed all of Pakistan's Northern
Areas[1] for high-altitude porters. In the end, no fewer than

sixty men were hired from Gojal, Hunza, Nagar, and Baltistan. It speaks for everybody's stamina that they succeeded in establishing as many as three high camps. However, the cold and the increasingly unbearable weather conditions enervated both the members and HAPs. Nobody felt enthusiastic for a summit bid. On the contrary, the HAPs suddenly began to abandon the expedition in droves. Rajab says that the ones eventually left included his friend Mohabbat, a man from Hunza, and himself. This afforded them a considerable monetary reward, which was rupees 15,000 each. However, collecting the numerous tents and other equipment from the high camp sites was a challenge without the HAPs. Most of it was picked up by helicopter crews (altitude permitting)[2] and dropped at base camp, instead of being transported to Skardu. This was because the members' ambition had not been satisfied yet. They had decided to turn to Broad Peak as a substitute for their winter climb.

According to Rajab, for this purpose they had to apply for a permit with the then president of Pakistan, General Zia ul-Haq. This was because they could not bear to sit and wait for lengthy government procedures to be completed in the relentless conditions of the Karakoram winter. Two Poles did manage to summit Broad Peak, but one of them paid too high a price for it. He contracted such severe frostbite on both hands and feet that he could not walk without support. Rajab says that rather than prop him up, other members decided to carry him from camp 4 to camp 1. In camp 1, he and Mohabbat received him and carried him down to base camp. He was then shifted to a hospital in Skardu by helicopter.

I use this story to ask Rajab Shah about his view of winter expeditions on eight-thousand-metre peaks.

'Very big problem. Impossible to summit,' is his reply.

Even at the base camp, it is hard to survive the daily onslaught of winter. He considers winter expeditions a questionable thing.

It was in 1989 that Rajab celebrated his eight-thousand-metre peaks debut. The Pakistan Army expedition on Nanga Parbat, which Mohammad Ullah has reported on, made him and Rajab Shah the first Pakistanis to reach the summit of the Killer Mountain. He denies it when I ask him whether this ineradicable soubriquet caused him concern or even anxiety. On the contrary, he even broke trail above camp 4 on a summit day marred by bad weather. Since Mohammad Ullah has already given me details of this expedition, I spare Rajab further questions. I have a feeling that after the scores of interviews he has had to give during the course of his career as a HAP, he is tired of the interrogation and would like to keep the thing short and concise. This does not mean that he becomes impatient or less genial. It is just that he has more important things on his mind nowadays than answering interview questions. Consequently, I just get brief facts of Rajab's successes from 1990 to 1993.

In 1990, he reached the summit of Gasherbrum-I in brilliant weather with a Japanese group. He adds that everything is easy in good weather. Two years later, he repeated this success with Meherban Shah.

With his younger friend, Meherban, he also joined a Japanese expedition to the seven-thousand-metre peak Momil Sar in 1991. They managed to summit the peak.

He made it to his third eight-thousand-metre summit in 1993, when he stood atop Broad Peak. At that time, he became acquainted with Nazir Sabir, who was his fellow HAP on Broad Peak. Rajab calls him a 'very close friend', with whom he has spent a lot of time.

The seven-thousand-metre peak Shispare has already been characterized as extremely difficult and dangerous by Meherban Shah. Rajab is quick to agree and he adds that compared with Shispare, Nanga Parbat and K-2 are 'easy'. Still, in 1994, three Japanese climbers reached the summit of Shispare. For Rajab, camp 4 was the terminus.

1995 is Meherban and Rajab's K-2 year. It was also one of the disastrous years on K-2, with eight fatalities in total, out of whom six people died on the one same day: 13 August. It was also on this occasion that the world-class English climber Alison Hargreaves met her death.

Rajab and Meherban had been hired by a Dutch team. Once again, snowfall had lasted for many days. Conditions were difficult, especially on the summit bid. Although I have learned from Meherban Shah that two Dutch climbers did reach the summit, when I ask Rajab whether they were strong mountaineers, he says that strong is a relative term. He remembers that they were indeed strong, but did not participate in blazing the trail. This was his and Meherban's task.

'[It was a] very big problem,' he says while indicating the level of accumulated snow with his hands, which was almost chest-high.

It is quite difficult to even imagine blazing a trail beyond 8,000 metres without supplementary oxygen at 3 a.m. According to Rajab, they set off at 5 p.m. and they arrived at the top after fourteen hours.

Somebody has contrived this analogy: if a climber assumes that in reaching a summit he has reached his goal or even completed his expedition, he can be likened to a swimmer who swims out in the ocean for hours and forgets or ignores that he will have to swim all the way back. Therefore, on a mountain, if you have not summitted by a fixed deadline, turning back is the single correct decision.

In Rajab's group, things could have developed in a frighteningly different manner. However, the weather must have been good enough for their late arrival on the summit and, moreover, for their prolonged descent. The two Shimshalis did not make it down to camp 4 until 10 p.m., the Dutch by midnight. Total exhaustion took hold of them after 19 hours of maximum performance in those hostile regions. It was Meherban's job to make tea and soup; Rajab confesses with a smile, 'I only sleep'. Even the two latecomers were provided with hot liquids by Meherban, which is something supremely to his credit.

The descent to the base camp went in a similarly split fashion. Rajab and Meherban completed it in a single day; the two Dutch took two days. While descending, they met dozens of climbers moving up. Shortly afterwards, all of them were hit by adverse weather conditions, so much so that the outcome was multiple deaths on K-2.

In the summer of 1996, Rajab Shah took part in the oft-quoted expedition to Passu Peak and summitted with his Shimshali friends. Once again, he uses the epithet 'easy'. I guess I can believe the likes of Rajab Shah.

The failed Everest expedition of 1997 is reported in Meherban Shah's chapter.

Rajab completed his eight-thousander quintet in 1998, when he made it to the top of G-II with three Japanese and another four high-altitude porters. It was probably easy.

What has so far been our subject is almost exclusively Rajab's eight-thousanders. It should not be omitted that he summitted Muztagh Ata twice, Mingli several times, and, with a women's expedition, Koksil Peak too.

For more than a decade now, he has not done any climbing but, as he stresses, he is a healthy retiree.

Towards the end of our interview, I ask him about the impact of the link road since its opening in 2003. What is his assessment of the progress that it has implied and the loss of many a tradition that is also connected with it?

He replies with his typical wisdom. He says that the older generation loves to criticize the younger ones and laments changes. He is not among the sceptics and objectors. Changes are a natural phenomenon; they come in each generation. And it is a good thing too to have changes. He used to cooperate with his peers, and today he wants to benefit the young in his role as a climbing instructor. He also expresses his positive view of the SMS, which he chairs. To him it means great progress; he loves to teach there.

Notes

1. Former name of Gilgit-Baltistan.
2. Helicopters can reach quite varying flight altitudes.

2.11

Syed Ahmed

High-altitude porter, date of birth unknown

ALTHOUGH SYED AHMED DOES NOT BELONG TO THE OLDER
generation, by any means, he still cannot name his date of
birth. We try to resolve this for him and agree on around 1967
because Sarwar Ali (born 1967) was his classmate during the
single year that he attended school.

I know Syed's elder brother Nyamat Ullah and can hardly
believe that these two men are brothers. Nyamat is a teacher
and postmaster. His conduct is open and urbane, while
Syed comes across as an introverted person. While Nyamat's
English is quite good, his taciturn brother does not utter a
single word in this language. What adds colour to the interview
is his little daughter whom he keeps holding in his arms and
who sometimes demands his loving attention.

I know that this will be a concise interview. Syed does not
respond when I ask how he became a climber. It seems that
he followed Mohammad Ullah and Yousaf Khan when they
approached him out of the blue in 1995. Syed Ahmed was
neither a trained climber nor had any prior experience of
high-altitude climbing. He had been a winter shepherd with
the yaks thrice, and thus had experienced cold, snow, and
loneliness in the open. His first mountain was the 1995 joint

army expedition on Gasherbrum-II, where he reached camp 3.

During a three-year break he attended one of Rajab Shah's training sessions on Malangutti Glacier.

In 1998, he returned to Gasherbrum-II and made it up to camp 4.

The next year, Syed's expedition on K-2 was cancelled due to a fatal accident on the mountain. Then he proceeded to Spantik and summited the seven-thousand-metre high mountain along with six members. For the year 2001, he mentions an expedition to Gasherbrum-II with Rajab Shah, Meherban Shah, and Hazil Shah, which none of the others has mentioned. There is some confusion here. Some of the information that Syed provides is contradictory to what his colleagues say, whereas the latter are broadly in line with each other. I think it is better to conclude that Syed does not regard himself and his biography as terribly important. In order not to leave too many inconsistencies, I take the freedom to both adapt things to the others' reports and put a question mark if necessary.

Syed says that he was with Japanese climbers on K-2 in 2002. While they indeed reached the highest point, he stayed in camp 4. I inquire about the reason behind staying back. Was he too exhausted or high-altitude-sick? Had they denied the summit to him? To this, Syed blandly says, 'no motivation'. I am surprised but I also understand. There is no reward or public recognition for ascending this summit in Pakistan. The general indifference in public makes Syed shrug his shoulders. In no way will he take all the risks of a summit bid for absolutely nothing. He does not consider the idea of increased self-esteem, so the whole thing makes no sense to him.

In 2003, he went to an expedition on Gasherbrum-II and reached as far as camp 3.

In 2004, he was again on Gasherbrum-II with six Germans and one Japanese. The second camp had been fixed when the weather became bad. Some still wished to proceed although the group had run out of rope. New snow triggered an avalanche which killed three members. The body of one of them could not even be found. The other two dead bodies were 'buried' on the spot, i.e. they were lowered into a crevasse because, according to the leader, it would have been too costly to carry them down and take them to their native countries.

In 2005, Syed Ahmed was on Broad Peak with a group of five weak Greek climbers, who had to stop at camp 2 because they could not climb any further than that.

Syed Ahmed's breakthrough came when he summited Gasherbrum-II in 2006 with a Serbian team and a Balti HAP. He does not give me any details of this expedition.

The following year, he was with Japanese climbers on Tirich Mir, the highest mountain of the Hindu Kush (North West Frontier Province)[1] They succeeded in climbing Dilgurzum (6,600m).

In 2008, he was part of an international expedition to Gasherbrum-II. Bad weather forced the climbers back from camp 3.

In 2009, he was on Broad Peak with a French expedition. They managed to make it to camp 4.

In 2010, he was again with the French on Broad Peak. This time, two climbers summited the mountain.

In 2011, he went to Broad Peak once more and witnessed the fatal fall of the Chinese, which Aziz Baig has told me about.

In 2012, he undertook his fourth expedition to Broad Peak, and then a trip to K-2 with ten Australians. On Broad Peak, the climb ended at camp 4 due to bad weather, and at camp 2 on K-2.

I don't learn anything else beyond this.

At the end of the interview, I feel it is futile to try and get a story of any kind from Syed Ahmed. I regret not being able to add more colour to his personality; the reader will have to do without it.

Note

1. Today renamed as Khyber-Pakhtunkhwa.

2.12

Ezat Ullah Baig

High-altitude porter, born 1970

WHEN SAMAD AND I ARRIVE AT EZAT ULLAH BAIG'S HOUSE
at the appointed hour, he sends us away. We do not learn why.
We are told to come again at four o'clock the next day.

He is a rather stout and solid type, and looks a bit older
than his forty-two years.

Ezat suffered a severe setback due to a mysterious illness
that hit him in 2005 at the base camp of Gasherbrum-II. He
says he had some sort of a 'panic attack', which disturbed
and troubled him even on the way back to Skardu. Upon his
arrival in Skardu, he went to the hospital and was diagnosed
with a strange condition which he calls 'water in the brain'.
The case was severe enough to refer him to the Combined
Military Hospital (CMH) in Rawalpindi, and eventually to the
renowned AKU (Aga Khan University) Hospital in Karachi.
The doctors prescribed various medicines that he had to take
for no less than three years.

People around him intimate that it was a psychosis. I learn
that his character has undergone a metamorphosis. Whereas
he used to be an easygoing and unpretentious individual,
today he tends to react in an unpredictable and sometimes
intemperate manner.

During the interview, there will be some confusing moments for me but otherwise we get along just fine.

In 2006, a year after this crisis, he once again tried to work as a HAP on Broad Peak. Much to his regret, he had to leave after a week because he felt sick at the base camp.

From the way he spreads his large photo collection on the floor, I deduce that quitting the job must have been a hard decision for him to take. He seems to revel in them, in a nostalgic and pleased fashion. He can hardly stop selecting the photos and talking about them one after the other, so I am at a loss with how to draw his attention towards the interview and away from the photos.

Unlike his inexhaustible comments on the photos, when it comes to describing his expeditions, he does not give many details, not to mention that some of this information is also questionable.

Ezat Ullah Baig attended school in Shimshal for eight years, followed by two years in Karachi. His father Bahti Bai played a significant role in the village. He was chairman of the road construction committee, which AKRSP[1] installed in 1985 for the local coordination of the building process. However, it was not granted to Bahti Bai to witness the completion of the link road in 2003. He contracted leukaemia and died in the AKU Hospital in Karachi. His mortal remains were taken from Gilgit by helicopter for burial in Shimshal.

It took Rajab Shah and Meherban Shah's training offers on Malangutti Glacier to attract Ezat to climbing.

In 1995, he joined a Spanish team for Sonia Peak. Two years later, a Japanese team hired him for a mountain that he says is in 'Bagrot'. He cannot recall its name. It was probably the seven-thousand-metre peak, Dhiran.

In the summer of 2000, he went to Gasherbrum-II with

an Italian group and tried to climb it from the Chinese side. According to him, it is a difficult route which requires technical climbing. They had established camp 1 and descended to base camp when an avalanche swept away camp 1 altogether. The expedition was then abandoned. However, he stayed with the Italians and wandered around with them on Concordia for three months visiting the base camps of each eight-thousand-metre peak in that proximity.

His eight-thousand-metre summit success came on Gasherbrum-II, when he ascended the mountain with a Greek expedition from its Skardu side. He was then requested by his tour operator ATP to linger in base camp and be ready for another group (French), with whom he made it to camp 3.

Ezat Ullah Baig also worked on K-2 in 2002 with a team of climbers from Spain. They had just proceeded to the first camp when an avalanche hit the group. They called off the expedition because a high-altitude porter from Chilas had died. He had not fastened his karabiner properly and was torn away by the avalanche. Ezat and Meherban Shah, who was with an American team, carried the dead body to advanced base camp where a helicopter was expected to pick it up. What followed was a futile wait of four days. In the end, the deceased had to be transported to Concordia where, on the fifth day, his body could be collected and flown out.

About the summer of 2003, Ezat Ullah reports that there was a whole lot of new snow, so much so that the provision of food from Skardu to the base camps could not be accomplished by the low porters alone. Supplies had to be delivered by helicopter. The snowfall also prevented Ezat's group from ascending beyond camp 2 on Gasherbrum-II.

He narrates that in 2004, three Shimshalis—Qudrat Ali, Meherban Karim, and himself—reached the summit of

Gasherbrum-II. According to him, it was an ATP-organized expedition with Ralf Dujmovits and Gerlinde Kaltenbrunner. However, from Qudrat Ali I learn that in 2004 he was not on Gasherbrum-II but on Gasherbrum-I, and so were Gerlinde and Ralf.

Ezat Ullah contradicts and maintains, 'No, it was Gasherbrum-II.'

He adds that on this expedition, Meherban Karim fell in a crevasse, which was 100 metres deep while descending. I believe I have misheard. Does he mean one hundred feet? Probably not, as he is certain and vehemently insists on one hundred metres. He says that young Karim was on the rope and did not suffer any injuries but it took Qudrat and him ninety minutes to rescue him from the crevasse. He describes the procedure in minute detail but neither Samad nor I are able to comprehend anything.

It looks like the end of the interview now as we have approached the fateful year of 2004.

After his failed attempt to restart his HAP career in 2006, Ezat Ullah has only joined trekking groups.

Note

1. Aga Khan Rural Support Programme.

2.13

Sabs Ali

High-altitude porter, date of birth unknown

SABS ALI IS THE YOUNGER BROTHER OF SHIMSHAL'S DOCTOR, Farman Ullah, and their resemblance is remarkable; however, Farman Ullah speaks English almost fluently, whereas Sabs Ali does not. His year of birth is not certain but is assumed to be 1961. Like Ezat Ullah Baig, he is Qudrat Ali's brother-in-law. Qudrat Ali has three sisters.

In 2010, he became the grandfather of a wonderful boy, Mohammad Sufi, who is with us during the interview. The child behaves well throughout; only towards the end he begins to complain and pull away.

Sabs Ali says that he went to school for three years. It was during the times of the well-known Ghulam Sultan from Gulmit, thus in an age where students had to do without paper and pen and used home-made slates of wood or stone and white 'ink'.

Sabs Ali tells me that in the 1970s, Australians passed through Shimshal to visit the seven-thousand-metre peak Yukshin Gardan. On their way back to Shimshal and Passu, he worked for them as a teenage porter and as part of this job, left his native village for the first time.

In 1995, Sabs Ali joined Rajab Shah's climbing class on

Malangutti. He lists the other participants that included Aziz Baig, Farhad Khan, Amin Ullah Baig, Amruddin, and Qurban Mohammad. Besides Rajab, the other two instructors were Meherban Shah and Tafat Shah. He adds that the two young friends Qudrat Ali and Shaheen Baig could already be considered teachers rather than students.

It was on Gasherbrum-II that Sabs Ali had his first experience as a high-altitude porter. He says that it was in 1999, although when I compare his details and names with those of the other HAPs, I conclude that it must have been 1998. Rajab Shah and Meherban Shah, who, he says, were his fellow high porters, were on Gasherbrum-II in 1998, and the same is true for Aziz Baig. It must have been one of the two large Japanese expeditions. Sabs Ali recalls eighteen members and twenty HAPs. Due to the magnitude of the undertaking, they contrived a climbing tactic that divided the group into three smaller units. Rajab and Meherban joined the first one and indeed reached the summit of Gasherbrum-II. They returned to the base camp and assisted the second unit, which was halted at camp 4 by the onset of unfavourable weather. My inquiries about further details and events, and feats and failures on the mountain remain unanswered.

I must add that the day of Sabs Ali's interview coincided with his family's threshing days, which is the busiest time of the year. Moreover, I somehow sense that my current interviewee hardly considers himself a high-altitude porter by profession. He rather identifies himself with what is his prevailing occupation in Shimshal. He is an interior designer, i.e. he gives his advice and assistance in the composition and style of the interior of rooms and helps with the decoration of wooden pillars and beams.

Though he likes to identify himself as an interior designer, the fact remains that he has stood atop an eight-thousand-metre peak. It was in the year 2000 that he was taken along to an expedition on Gasherbrum-II by his brother-in-law, Qudrat Ali. Qudrat recommended him to Ralf Dujmovits, who was leading a team of twelve German climbers. Qudrat and Ralf did the trail-blazing and rope-fixing work. With five or six group members, Ralf, Qudrat, and Sabs Ali summited Gasherbrum-II.

A year later, he was once again hired as a HAP on Gasherbrum-II—this time also by Germans. The group was prevented by bad weather from proceeding beyond camp 3.

From then onwards, he has confined his activities to trekking tours around Shimshal, with one exception.

It was in 2008 when he worked for Koreans who planned to climb the seven-thousand-metre peak, Batura-II. The trek to base camp started in Hassanabad in the Hunza Valley. The expedition was to last for six weeks. The four Baturas (also called 'Batura Wall') are known for a high risk of avalanches. When the team arrived at the base camp, they met a number of low porters coming from Batura-I base camp. Their faces indicated shock and dejection as all members of their Japanese expedition had been killed by an avalanche.

Of Sabs Ali's team, two climbers reached the summit of Batura-II.

After covering his climbing career, I wonder whether at the end of the interview, he would like to make some remarks on his village, and on current or future developments. Would he like to praise or criticize? Does he have ideas? What comes to his mind regarding his native Shimshalis?

Initially, he expresses general contentment. Then he goes on to stress how important it is for a functioning community to have the members of the relevant committees and boards cooperate in an honest and unselfish manner. I try to read between the lines and realize that there might be something amiss here. I poke around a bit and ask about his views on the Shimshal Nature Trust (SNT).

When, in 1997, the SNT was founded in cooperation with the Canadian David Butz, its original goal was conservation. Meanwhile, it has extended its activities and influence in other areas and proudly calls itself an 'umbrella organization', but this certainly does not garner everybody's appreciation.

Sabs Ali declines to comment on it. His son Kalim, an educated young man and father of little Mohammad Sufi, is the Mayor Shaheen Karim's first secretary and often has to deal with the SNT. I do not wish to pry too much into this topic so we shake hands and I leave him in peace.

2.14

Meherban Karim

High-altitude porter, born 1978, died 2008

THE YOUNGEST OF MY CLIMBERS HAS ALREADY PASSED away. It still moves his widow Haji Parveen and others to tears. Nevertheless, she assures me that I can interview her. To me it is akin to causing considerable botheration to someone. After all, how much can I ask and in what detail? Will I reopen wounds which have not yet healed?

I knew Meherban Karim very well. His family—comprising a wife and three children, Umbreen, Ibrar, and Raheem—lived right next to the house of Qudrat Ali and Lal Paree, who were my hosts in 2003 and 2004.

Karim always wore a bright smile on his face. This image of him is indelibly imprinted in my memory. Besides his duties as a father (his eldest daughter Umbreen was born when he was just twenty years old), he had other interests, one of which became clear when, in February 2004, he tinkered with an old mountain bike and then jolted across the bare wintry fields on it.

It was his passion for adventure that took him to climbing. This becomes unequivocally clear through Parveen's narrative. What the reader cannot expect of her, and understandably so, are the numbers of years that Meherban dedicated to this activity and other hard facts. However, from her words, he comes across as an individual who is more energetic and vigorous than many climbers I met in person.

Haji Parveen says that Karim was enchanted with Qudrat and Shaheen's climbing zeal. These two knew how to make climbing look fascinating and heroic because of their technical skills and expertise. It is no wonder then that Karim also wished to give it a try. Parveen says that Karim had heard of Rajab Shah's training sessions on Malangutti Glacier, but he did not attend them.

Daredevil as he was, he simply began climbing one day. Haji Parveen does not remember the year but the destination was Broad Peak. Qudrat took him along. It must have been the year 1999. She recalls being a bystander, feeling helpless and alone while he was packing his rucksack. They had been married for three years and little Umbreen was sleeping in her cradle nearby. Eventually, she became comfortable with it and began to follow the packing process with more expertise. She used to check if he had kept enough batteries for his headlamp, or packed the lighter and a replacement for it, in addition to his sunglasses and a second pair for an emergency.

Haji Parveen believes that her husband reached the summit of Broad Peak. She says that climbing had become his passion. He talked incessantly about the challenge and euphoria that he felt while climbing. I can imagine only too well how afraid she was for this easygoing, amiable man. At times, she would try to dissuade and prevent him from going but it all went in vain. To all her pleas, he would just say that he did not share her worries, just as if he were inviolable. His optimism was boundless.

Meherban Karim reached four eight-thousander summits. He stood atop Gasherbrum-I in 2004 with Qudrat

Ali and Ezat Ullah Baig. He reached the summit of Nanga Parbat twice, which was a huge achievement for such a young man.

I do not learn anything about the Nanga Parbat expeditions from his wife. I have read about his last and fatal climb on K-2. There is evidence that on 1 August 2008 he stood on the highest point of the 'King of Mountains'. Unfortunately, this 'success' ended in ultimate failure for him.

Karim and his client, Hugues d'Aubarède, were probably a fatal pair. They were a team of an old and a young man, who came together for their insatiable desire to summit K-2 and as a result lost their lives.

As described in Meherban Shah's chapter, the 61-year-old Frenchman was a headstrong, or rather obsessive, climber who could not be deterred from his dream of summiting K-2. This is also documented in Graham Bowley's book *No Way Down*. In 2008, d'Aubarède had engaged his friend Qudrat Ali as a guide on K-2. Qudrat had also brought along Meherban Karim as a high-altitude porter. Like dozens of other K-2 aspirants, d'Aubarède had been confined to the base camp by unfavourable weather for no less than nineteen days. He was about to cancel his expedition and abandon his dream, all the more since Qudrat had to leave him on account of another engagement. He had already made arrangements for his untimely departure when suddenly the ultimate chance was offered to him: he could join a Dutch team. With that, he took the risk of climbing without his experienced guide Qudrat. He contented himself with Meherban Karim, who was not hard to win over, and managed to hire another Shimshali, Jehan Baig, for his ambitious purpose.

The fact that d'Aubarède and Karim indeed reached the top of K-2 is proven by a photograph in Bowley's book. The book also establishes that during the entire climb d'Aubarède was on the edge of collapse. How is someone, who is at the end of his tether, has not made it to the summit until evening, and has also run out of supplementary oxygen, supposed to return without massive help from another person?

Haji Parveen believes that her husband sacrificed his life for the Frenchman. I guess Karim was well aware of what high-altitude porters are expected to do in this kind of crisis. It is quite possible that he would have reached the summit early enough to return to camp 4 had he not felt responsible for Hugues. However, this is speculation. We are in the dark about the circumstances of the two men's deaths.

This ambiguity about the circumstances of Karim's death is most painful for Haji Parveen, and is a major reason why she cannot put her mind at ease. She does not know about the exact spot where Karim died on this horrible mountain, and when and how. Was it a rapid death? A merciful one? What was he thinking in his last moments? And where is he now because he must be somewhere, mustn't he?

At this point, she bursts into sobs. She had tried to talk him out of this K-2 adventure and had pleaded with him not to go.

Today, Parveen lives off a little shop in Shimshal that she established in order to survive. She is also supported by her network of family and friends.

2.15

Yousaf Khan

Soldier in retirement, born 1954

IT REQUIRED EXTRA STAMINA AND PATIENCE TO GET HOLD of Yousaf Khan for an interview. When I first inquired about him, I learned that he was sojourning in Islamabad with his eldest son, Sahib, so I postponed my visit until after his return. As soon as I heard of his arrival, I went to Khizerabad, where I met him in the dust of hard work. He was in the midst of harvesting wheat. Even then we made an appointment for the following day; however, it did not materialize. One of his younger sons came to me to inform me that his father had left for Pamir to help with *Kooch*, i.e. migration from one summer settlement to another. I knew that this would keep him unavailable for at least one week.

I became quite hopeful on his return, but he sent a message informing me that he would be needed on his nephew's Zulfikar Ali's wedding. After that, he would have to escort his daughter-in-law Maheen to Hunza, where she was to give birth to her first child.

The wedding went as planned but the baby didn't. It wanted to be born prematurely. The transport had just reached Gulmit when Maheen was delivered and the next day they came back to Shimshal.

A day later, I have the opportunity to see the newborn girl, offer my greetings to the young mother, and finally interview the grandfather, Yousaf Khan.

He has set aside photos and even made notes of his expeditions in the notebook of his youngest son to prop his memory. During the interview, he often consults these notes in order to confirm the years of his expeditions; however, specific dates do not always seem correct.

Yousaf Khan attended school from grade one to five in Shimshal. Among his class fellows were Rajab Shah, Mohammad Ullah, and Farman Ullah who was the youngest and the most gifted student.

Unlike some of my older interviewees, I learn from Yousaf Khan that besides Urdu or Pakistan Studies, the students were taught Geography and Islamiat. I also hear for the first time that prior to Daulat Amin there was a Shimshal-born teacher named Mohammad Nayab. The others had only mentioned Ghulam Sultan of Gulmit. Yousaf praises Mohammad Nayab's commitment towards his students and adds that his father, Ghulam Nasir, was the right-hand man of Hunza's Mir.[1]

Yousaf Khan first left Shimshal on the same yak trek that carried supplies from Shimshal to the Mir of Hunza. He says that even the modest village of Gulmit on the KKH appeared alien to him. He had an uncle there, whose comprehensive knowledge and intellectual superiority deeply impressed the young Shimshali. This was what he also wanted to achieve, but the money which would have enabled his family to pay for his education was not there.

From Yousaf Khan, I learn some more interesting details of the 1963 Khurdapin disaster. The Khurdapin Glacier, located approximately 20 kilometres upstream from Shimshal, had pushed across the valley of the Shimshal River and dammed the latter in such a way that a vast lake had developed. It was expected that, sooner or later, the dam would burst and thus send unimaginable masses of water, icebergs, and moraine debris down onto Shimshal. There was a small army unit stationed in the village at that time, which helped to take precautions against the looming catastrophe.

Yousaf Khan was then a nine-year-old boy. In the summer holidays, he tended sheep and goats with his mother in Yazben, which means that they were staying between the lake and Shimshal, precisely on the route of the impending flood. He relates that they were notified and warned of the flood threat by someone who was passing by. In great haste, the mother and son strode along towards the village fifteen kilometres downstream, first across the snow-white Yazghil Glacier, then along the Shimshal River on rough terrain. Three days later, the cataclysm became a reality. What Yousaf chiefly recalls is the noise—the rumbling, booming, roaring noise—which seemed to be going on forever and bringing total annihilation. The soldiers had evacuated the neighbourhood along the river called Khan Area, and moved the inhabitants to more elevated parts of the village. Moreover, a security zone had been set up, which could not be entered by anybody.

Although the extent of material damage was enormous, thanks to the precautionary measures taken well ahead of time, there were no human casualties. However, forty years later, in 2003, when I first cast a glance at Khan Area—still an empty and desolate expanse—the very idea of the catastrophe sent shivers down my spine. The construction work in the last ten years has resulted in the establishment of a school, kindergarten, and a teachers' house to name just a few. It looks like the four glaciers upstream have sworn an oath to remain still.

The soldiers who were present in Shimshal during the flood attracted extra attention from the older and younger boys of the village. This could be one of the several important reasons why Yousaf Khan chose to become a soldier. A career in the army was some sort of substitute for the higher education which was denied to him. Then there were also the factors of a regular income and retirement benefits. Last, but not the least, Yousaf says that the army protects his country, which is why it pleases him to be a member of the military.

He applied to the army in 1972. Sixteen years were to pass before he started high-altitude climbing as a soldier. Indeed, as a military man, he did practise on the mountainous terrain, crossed glaciers, and learned to ski and climb, but that was on comparatively lower mountains of up to 6,000 metres. All of the equipment, from tent to ice screws, came from European sources as was already mentioned by Mohammad Ullah, whereas the instructors were Pakistani.

The first serious high-altitude expedition, according to Yousaf Khan, took place in 1988 on Sia Kangri (7,422m) in the Baltoro region. He believes that it was a virgin mountain but John Mock in his book *Lonely Planet* has provided different information. As early as 1934, an international expedition had reached the summit of this mountain. In 1988, of the ten army members, five made it to the top and Yousaf Khan was among them. He says he fixed ropes in difficult places in cooperation with Flight Lieutenant Mohammad Atta. The weather on summit day was altogether unfavourable, which is why the success of the effort is even more commendable.

In 1989, the army launched the Nanga Parbat expedition that Mohammad Ullah and Rajab Shah have talked about. Besides the leaders Colonel Sher Khan and Flight Lieutenant Mohammad Atta, Yousaf also names Captain Iqbal as one of the participants. These men were educated enough to communicate with a German climber who had joined them. Despite the adverse weather conditions, the German climber managed to reach the summit. Yousaf stayed in camp 4 on summit day.

A year later, he reached the highest point of Gasherbrum-I. It was a joint expedition of the French and Pakistani armies. The group comprised eight Frenchmen and five Pakistanis, including Yousaf Khan and Mohammad Ullah. The communication was mainly done in English. Two Pakistanis and three Frenchmen managed to ascend to the summit. Yousaf says that the weather was excellent that day. It was mostly sunny from base camp to the very top and back again too. Before the eyes of the marvelling Pakistanis, one of the Frenchmen unpacked his paraglider and flew down to base camp.

In 1991, a Pakistani-German military expedition to Broad Peak led Yousaf to become friends with Dr Alfred Thomas, a German army doctor from Koblenz. This expedition was meant to facilitate clinical research into the phenomenon of high-altitude sickness, which hasn't been fully understood to date. Consequently, the focus was less on a summit ambition and more on medical examinations, quantifications, and evaluations taken from the twelve Pakistani and German participants. Yousaf says that the team had started to measure each member's data in Rawalpindi (which is only at an altitude of 600 metres), and his results were excellent.

After the medical expedition was over, Dr Thomas visited Yousaf Khan's family thrice in Shimshal. In addition to strengthening their friendship, these visits were aimed at mountaineering—in 2004, Dr Thomas and some German friends successfully climbed the six-thousander Yazghil Sar east of Shimshal for the first ever time—and a project that was supposed to make the use of solar energy popular in Shimshal. Dr Thomas had correctly identified that the village was really backward in terms of the knowledge and utilization of solar energy. He became active and brought along two solar cookers from Germany in 2004. One of these cookers was for Yousaf's family and the second for the community. Although they were bulky appliances, they could have been properly used. Yousaf says that he sporadically uses his cooker to boil water. However, the community-owned cooker has been stashed away and forgotten.

Alfred Thomas invited Yousaf's eldest son, Sahib, in 2007 to Germany for four months and sponsored a course in the German language for him.

Some time later, Dr Thomas was diagnosed with a brain tumour. Despite, or because of this appalling certainty, he travelled to Shimshal in 2008 for the last time. He died on 24 October 2009.

With a multi-national expedition, Yousaf Khan was once again on Broad Peak in 1994. The members included five Americans, eight Pakistanis, two Frenchmen, and three Italians. According to Yousaf, they made it to camp 4, but the summit bid was thwarted by unfavourable weather.

Yousaf succeeded in reaching his second eight-thousander summit, Gasherbrum-II, in 1995. This time, he was part of a joint expedition of eight Pakistanis, three Italians, and three Canadians. The leader of this expedition was the Pakistani, Lieutenant Colonel Pirzada. He says it was only the expedition's Pakistani members who reached the top, and among them were two high-altitude porters from Skardu.

In 1996, he climbed Masherbrum (7,821m) with a Pakistan Army expedition.

In their reports, Mohammad Ullah and Aziz Baig
had mentioned Yousaf Khan as a member of the 1997
Pakistani-Chinese expedition to Nanga Parbat, but he says
nothing about it. I do not wish to prod him into revealing
anything he doesn't want to share. He was evidently not
among the summiteers.

Yousaf Khan's last expedition was in 2002. This was the
climbing expedition to Sunrise Peak near Shimshal, which
Hazil Shah has already talked about in his chapter. Yousaf's
report differs from Hazil's, who depicts himself both as the
initiator and leader of the tour.

It is correct that Hazil was the initiator of the expedition.
Yousaf says that Hazil had negotiated this tour with the Alpine
Club of Pakistan and got it registered as a first climb to
Sunrise Peak, which resulted in a small financial contribution
from the Club's side. Hazil made these arrangements and kept
quiet about them. Not until he had completed the preliminary
work did he address potential members and won over thirteen
Shimshalis for this first climb. However, Yousaf does not agree
with Hazil's claim of being the leader of the expedition. He
says that the leader was not Hazil, but Rajab Shah and himself.

The year 2002 also marks the end of Yousaf's military
service. After thirty years, he retired as a *Subedar*[2] and now
receives a monthly pension of around eight-thousand rupees.

His family, especially his wife, like to refer to him as *Subedar*
instead of calling him by his real name.

Notes

1. Persian equivalent of Prince.
2. Rank in Pakistan Army, equivalent to that of a Captain.

2.16

Ali Musa

Climber, born 1967

ALI MUSA'S INTERVIEW IS CONDUCTED IN KARIMABAD, Hunza, where he has lived since 2004 with his wife and three children. He is one of the first Shimshalis to settle permanently in Hunza. I have long since announced my visit and noticing his readiness and fluency, I can safely conclude that he has prepared beforehand for the interview. There are obviously some important issues which he has planned to communicate and point out. His English is by far the best of all my interviewees, hence I don't require Samad's assistance. He is articulate and employs a wide range of vocabulary in a way that is quite similar to that of other Shimshalis, especially the young ones. However, he often switches from one period of his life to another, so I have problems sorting out the chronology of his report.

Ali Musa is Yousaf Khan's nephew, and although he belongs to the younger climbers, the year of his birth is not certain. He was probably born in 1967. I know both, his immediate family—his wife Aziza and children Shahana, Nazakat, and Samir—and the wider family, i.e. his mother Zaibul Nisa, his seven siblings, and his four uncles and their families. They are one of Shimshal's ambitious and high-flying clans. Some members have already presented themselves on the Internet with brightly coloured pictures and eloquent texts.

As the eldest brother, at age sixteen and after his father's premature death, it was Ali Musa's foremost duty to take care of his siblings. He had to quit school and go to Islamabad to earn money in one way or the other. From the start he was inclined to engage in mountain tourism. He has achieved this goal in a convincing manner. Looking at his numerous contacts, his ample knowledge, and clear viewpoints, one gets the impression that he could be an excellent driving force behind Pakistani mountain tourism and contribute to providing a better structure and national standing.

However, there was an incident which seemed to thwart such a career. A car hit him in Karachi and smashed both his shinbone and fibula. The doctors who treated this fracture (he pulls up his jeans and points at an uneven and scarred spot) instantly predicted the end of his mountaineering career. The treatment took four months, and Ali Musa had to spend two of them as an in-patient. His bones had to be patched up with metal parts. The doctors told him that he should, on no account, pursue the idea of climbing.

However, Ali Musa thrived and proved the doctors wrong. Through climbing, not only did he finance his two brothers' education, but also bought a flashy jeep for another brother, Madad, who is now earning good money as a driver on the link road between Shimshal and Passu.

As he calls it, his 'climbing biography' began in October 1995 in Shimshal. With two other teenagers, Ali Musa had set his mind to climbing the snow-covered Shifktin Sar, a five-thousand-metre peak in Shimshal's immediate neighbourhood. From the way he relates this episode, I get a truly vivid idea of these three lads—Ali Musa, Qudrat Ali, and Shaheen Baig—

and their dreams and boundless energy that enabled them to embark on this climb. Half in earnest and half with irony—as if they had already been seasoned climbers—he continuously says 'we discussed, we made a plan'. They were also short of equipment. They begged it of Rajab Shah, Mohammad Ullah, and Uncle Yousaf Khan. They did not even know how to handle these things, but the very colours, the gaudy brightness of the borrowed jackets, and the clink of the metal was sufficient to send them over the moon. The mountain fever kept them awake until late in the night.

'We discussed the route, and the spot for the high camp, and other things like where do we put on the crampons. How do we use the ice axes.' Ali Musa recalls.

All of this happened while the community was busy with *Kooch*, the annual return of the livestock from the high pastures. Understandably so, it was with mild scepticism rather than enthusiasm that the villagers were observing the three juniors. However, even then, as Ali Musa claims, everybody watched as they set off from Aminabad, climbed along the slope, and pitched their tent on a perfectly visible spot. A meeting was held there from which Shaheen Baig and Ali Musa emerged as members and Qudrat Ali as the leader of the expedition. A lot of cooking and discussion was happening, and they were not sleeping much. Early in the morning, they enjoyed admiring each other in their beautiful boots and suits, and with their stylish sunglasses covering half their faces. They strapped on the crampons and tied a fifty-metre rope around their waists. Then they started placing the ice axes with great determination. It took them four or five hours to make a route in the quite deep snow until they did reach the summit of Shifktin Sar.

Not much later, Ali Musa first visited Skardu and was

amazed to see the crowds of foreigners there. They were all in their brightly coloured jackets and pants, and all of them were evidently mesmerized by the mountains. This was what he wanted to experience too.

In 1998, he travelled to Islamabad with his cousin Hazil Shah and registered with Nippa Travel[1] as a high-altitude porter. It was a coincidence that at this very point, the renowned Gasherbrum-II expedition which included the film team of the Japanese TV channel NHK, was about to set off. Ali Musa and Hazil Shah were hired as camera assistants. Seven hundred low porters (Hazil's figure was one thousand) hiked to the base camp, and twenty men from Shimshal and Skardu were engaged as HAPs. Although neither he nor Hazil reached the summit, Ali Musa recalls the tour as an important experience. For the first time, he got acquainted with the complete technical equipment. On the other hand, the tour was an eye-opener for him about a certain permanent companion of any high-altitude climber: death.

He first learned about the vulnerability of human life on mountains during the ascent, somewhere around camp 2. Wisps of fog kept obstructing everybody's vision. Hardly ever did the climbers raise their eyes. They stared at their own boot tips. Then suddenly Ali Musa saw something dark sticking out of the snow, barely three metres ahead of him. He thought that it was an abandoned tent and was about to push away the snow. At this moment, a Japanese climber behind him said, 'Leave it. It is a corpse.'

The man apparently knew this because he had been on the mountain twice. The deceased remained at the same spot; nobody retrieved the dead body. He was lying there as a writing on the wall for every climber. His corpse was a reminder of the mortality of human life.

It was not a small shock for the young Ali Musa; however, more was to come. The very next day, bad weather and low visibility engulfed the mountain once again. Nevertheless, the climb to camp 3 had begun. After walking for about a hundred metres, he saw a boot and a crampon in the ice. Rajab Shah explained to the novice that the rest of the dead body was buried deep in the ice; therefore, only one foot could be seen.

Involuntarily, he had a vision of himself lying in the snow, deserted and without any dignity, frozen into ice, and becoming an object of terror. 'What have I gotten into? Do I really want to be a climber?' He thought.

However, it was quite pointless to mull over these questions now and he had no choice but to continue and concentrate on his next step and nothing else. He had to suppress all other thoughts, especially the ones borne out of fear.

This pretty much points out the basic situation of a high-altitude climber. The mountain expeditions are a constant walk on a tightrope between courage and fear, carelessness and caution, and death and life.

Broad Peak was the first eight-thousander which Ali Musa summited. In 2000, he joined the famous Japanese climber Nazuka Hidagi, who was later killed by an avalanche on the Nepalese eight-thousander, Manaslu. Ali Musa does not share the details of this expedition, nor do I bother him with my questions about it. In the course of the interview, it becomes clear that Ali Musa sees himself as someone who has climbed the social ladder among his fellow HAPs. He states that it is because he is a freelance guide and gets hired by various tour operators. If necessary, he also works as a trekking guide, since guiding is his only source of income.

After his success on Broad Peak, he was interviewed by a

TV reporter, which was something special at that time. He felt proud to be questioned about his experiences on the mountain. He was also occasionally appointed as a liaison officer by the Alpine Club of Pakistan. For a long time, I have wondered why those enigmatic liaison officers have to join expeditions. I can hardly imagine a more dispensable and superfluous figure than the liaison officer on a mountain expedition. The two individuals I experienced personally (in 1997 on Muztagh Ata and in 2003 on Spantik) seemed to have no duties other than idly sitting around in the base camp and getting bored. Moreover, they were by no means awe-inspiring characters in uniform, as their names seemed to suggest. On the first occasion in China, the liaison officer was an anaemic youth who was addicted to computer games and, at night, liked to read us chapters from the so-called 'Mao Bible'. On the other occasion, the liaison officer was a well-intentioned comedian, who disappeared from the base camp every now and then and would not return until two or three days later.[2] Ali Musa explains that there are some so-called open areas and restricted areas. The liaison officer has to be an army member for the latter, while for the former, the tour operators can appoint their liaison officers as they wish. However, I do not find this a very convincing rationale for having a liaison officer on-board.

From his own 'climbing biography' on the Internet,[3] I learn that Ali Musa reached the summit of Gasherbrum-II in 2001. During the interview, he does not mention it. In the summer of 2002, he summited Muztagh Ata (7,546m) twice. He says that he was the first Pakistani to accomplish the double.

There are two exciting episodes from 2003 and 2012 that he wishes to narrate to me.

He was on Nanga Parbat in 2003 with a Japanese friend and his team. They had arrived at camp 2. Ali Musa set off alone for the descent to camp 1. It was already late in the afternoon.

He was right in the middle of a vertical passage when one of Nanga Parbat's infamous rock falls began. He was both lucky and unlucky. His good luck was that he remained unhurt. His misfortune became clear seconds later when he saw that the two fixed ropes had been severed and fallen off the wall. Moreover, his ice axe had been hit by a rock and jerked out of his hand. He was now clinging to the wall without his vital climbing tools.

As soon as he had somewhat recovered from his shock, he checked his situation but was, in the enveloping darkness, unable to discover anything that would have enabled him to continue climbing. There was no escape downward or upward, neither could he move left or right. A prisoner of the mountain, he was hanging in the vertical ice all alone. Ahead of him was the long, freezing night, which he thought he would never survive.

The new day was dawning and unexpectedly he was still alive, but his situation had in no way improved. He felt numb, dazed, and awfully stiff from desperately clinging to the mountain in extreme cold weather. He feared that his hands and feet were frostbitten.

Suddenly, something caught his eye that he hadn't been able to see in the night because of darkness. It was the end of a rope! Diagonally above him, a few metres away, the end of one of the torn ropes was dangling in the morning breeze.

'Do or die,' he said to himself loudly and firmly.

With his hands, he crawled to reach the end of the rope and managed to get hold of it. He also managed to tie some other pieces of the torn rope together, and finally rescued himself from the distressful situation.

His life had been saved but not his limbs: he had contracted frostbite. The expedition leader instantly sent him to Islamabad. He allotted his treatment just three days and like a true Shimshali, immediately returned to his team. The leader wrung his hands in desperation: 'Didn't I send you to Islamabad for recovery? How come you are already back?'

Ali Musa's response reveals his heroism.

He said, 'I love climbing. It is my job and my duty. Not until all of you decide to retreat will I also retreat. I will not desert you.'

The weather ultimately forced all of them to call off the expedition.

In 2012, he was on Broad Peak with a Chinese group. Five or six other teams were at that time besieging the mountain. Some of his group members had reached the third camp at 7,200 metres. Another team had erected their fourth camp at about 7,400 metres, but the location had not exactly been picked by experts. In other words, the tents were erected in a poorly chosen place.

As Ali Musa was ascending with his Chinese group members, they were suddenly faced with a strange spectacle. They saw a figure descending from the said camp 4 at a rapid speed. He was almost running. Something was not right with this person. The man seemed to hobble. One of his feet kept plunging deep in the snow. They wondered what was wrong. Ali Musa immediately realized that this person was wearing just one boot, while his other foot was wrapped in what seemed to be a plastic bag. What on earth had happened?

It emerged that an avalanche had whipped across this camp 4 during the night. The hapless guy said that parts of the equipment had been swept away or buried once and for all, including his left boot. Regrettably, his group did not have radio contact with the other camps (Ali Musa could not help noticing a certain consistent thoughtlessness there) and so his only option had been to stick his un-booted foot into a sleeping bag cover and hobble down as fast as possible.

He was allowed to use the radio of Ali Musa's group. The information about the untoward situation was communicated to base camp, so that his companions down there could send some help for him. One more bit of luck was accorded to the unlucky fellow as, in camp 2, he was accommodated by one of the numerous teams until in fact a pair of substitute boots arrived within an astonishing twenty-four hours.

Whether or not he was spared frostbite, Ali Musa does not know, since the good man had already left for Skardu when his team arrived at base camp.

In the course of our interview, Ali Musa repeatedly addresses the complex subject of the high-altitude porter's job, its background, work conditions, and the comparison with the Sherpas. Chapter III of this book is in large part based on his information and statements. He fervently speaks about the Pakistani HAPs' reputation. He says that the Sherpas are occasionally considered stronger than the Baltis, Shimshalis, and the men from Hunza. However, that is contrary to facts as Pakistani HAPs are stronger than them. The only thing working to their disadvantage is that they are isolated and bereft. In the words of Ali Musa, the HAPs do not get any 'technical support' and there is 'zero recognition' from the government's side. No official training system for HAPs exists. Each of them has to gain his skills and knowledge on his own from village elders such as Rajab Shah. Compared to the Sherpas' wages, the HAPs' pay is also puny.

According to Ali Musa, the problem is that the high-altitude porters speak little or no English and are therefore at a constant disadvantage when negotiating the job's terms. The uneducated high porters do not have firm and lasting business relations with tour operators like ATP or Nazir Sabir Expeditions. Thus, they are always in an inferior position and even susceptible to blackmail when payment is negotiated. Moreover, it does happen that one HAP undercuts the other, only to be the winner in the job race.

Ali Musa reiterates Moritz Steinhilber's observations that label Pakistani HAPs[4] as mercenaries.

> If someone puts his health and life at stake, like in the army or in high-altitude climbing, although he does not like doing it, but has to do so out of economic hardship, he is a mercenary. By saying this, I am not blaming the mercenaries but those who exploit their economic adversity. There is something massively rotten when such things happen, when the only thing you can offer is your own life.[5]

Ali Musa has long since relinquished the status of a mercenary, if he was ever one.

His conduct reflects the assertiveness of a self-made man. The modest prosperity he has achieved can be observed everywhere. His family lives in a meticulously clean rented house in the dream location of Karimabad. The children are wearing newly bought and certainly high-quality clothes. I am served a fine meal, and he receives several phone calls on his mobile, probably pertaining to business matters.

I am confident about Ali Musa and wish for him to be one of those who, in Gilgit-Baltistan's mountain tourism, will use their leverage for the betterment of high-altitude porters.

Notes

1. Pakistani tour operator with special affinity to Japan.
2. See also *Reflections on Liaison Officers* on www.sorenledet.com.au
3. Source: www.ismailimail.wordpress.com
4. ...and equally the Nepalese high-altitude porters from the Solu region, who have succeeded the affluent Sherpas.
5. Quoted from a private e-mail.

2.17

Jehan Baig

High-altitude porter, born *circa* 1976, died 2008

JEHAN BAIG WAS ONE OF THE TWO SHIMSHALIS WHO WERE among the eleven climbers killed on K-2 between 1–2 August 2008. The other was Meherban Karim, whose story has been covered already.

Samad and I meet his widow, Gul Dana, near the Jamaat Khana[1] and ask her as tactfully as possible if she is willing to answer our questions about her late husband. Like earlier with Haji Parveen, I do not feel comfortable asking her and expect her to decline our request. However, she does not refuse and kindly agrees. The next day we walk the two kilometres to her house in Aminabad. It is June, the fields are a lush green, the wild rose bushes along the way are abundant in blossoms, and release their fragrance in the breeze.

Gul Dana's family room is spotlessly tidied up. Along the wall adjacent to the entrance, there is a baby's cradle covered with a blanket. It is Ejaz Karim's little daughter who is slumbering there (see Hazil Shah's account about Sonia Peak).

It is not only Jehan Baig's widow who will answer our questions but also his mother, Naseeb Begum. She is small and fragile. Her soft but high-pitched voice reaches my heart.

When it comes to the circumstances of her son's death, she is unable to fight back her tears. In the end, both mother and daughter-in-law emphatically express their gratitude several times.

The late Jehan Baig had one brother, Ejaz Karim, and three sisters. He was the eldest son and thus responsible for all siblings. As a two-year-old toddler, he set off on a trip that was to keep him from Shimshal for four years. He was raised by his mother's family in Gulkin (a village between Gulmit and Passu on the KKH) until he was six.

Jehan Baig attended the Government School for Boys in Shimshal for five years. In his summer holidays, he annually walked the arduous way to the Pamir high pastures. Today you can still meet eight- or nine-year-olds who walk this three-day distance tirelessly, happily, and without a complaint, along with the adults. Judging by their speed, I am compelled to say that they don't walk, but run through the pastures. As a Westerner, I keep marvelling at their stamina and sure-footedness. Undoubtedly, it is here that the foundations are being laid for Shimshal's future HAPs.

Jehan Baig was thrice among the winter shepherds in Guijerav in the so-called 'Little Pamir'. The experience of enduring cold benefitted him later when he became a high-altitude porter.

When I ask about Jehan Baig's encounters with foreigners, I learn that he was already working as a porter for trekking groups during his teenage years because he had to earn money for his family.

As mentioned in Meherban Shah's chapter, Jehan Baig was oftentimes his companion on the mountain. Regrettably, there are now considerable differences between the places and dates which Meherban named and the ones about which

I learn from Gul Dana. For example, she does not mention any of the five K-2 expeditions on which her husband was supposedly Meherban's partner. Either Meherban, being a much older and also a very busy man, has jumbled some facts in his memory, or the widow has not been thoroughly informed about her late husband's activities.

According to Gul Dana, Jehan Baig started high-portering in 2004 after receiving the typical and brief climbing instructions from Rajab Shah and Meherban Shah. His first job was on Gasherbrum-II. Gul Dana says that the group was probably young and inexperienced, because none of the climbers had the slightest chance to make it to the summit. After several days of observing and waiting, Jehan and Meherban took the opportunity to join a different team and reached the summit. The reader will not find this mentioned in Meherban Shah's chapter.

I also want to know what chiefly motivated Jehan to pursue climbing. Was it for the reason of good money that he chose this vocation, or the challenge and love of adventure? Or was it the desire to excel in the climbing community?

Gul Dana insists that the monetary aspect was only of secondary importance. Jehan's top priority was to make a name for himself, his village Shimshal, the Ismaili community, and for Pakistan. With this attitude, it was impossible for him to forgo the chance of a summit bid, just because there was no bonus to earn, or because he shied away from additional toil and dangers. He was always content with his payment. Gul Dana never heard him complain; he always expressed his gratitude towards God for bestowing him with this source of income.

In 2005, Jehan Baig worked on Gasherbrum-I with Meherban Shah. Once again, we come through something that is not represented in Meherban's report. Gul Dana says that this time the members of the group were strong, hence he made it to the summit of this eight-thousander too.

Gul Dana also shares information about a K-2 expedition, to which Jehan went in 2006 with Meherban Shah. Unfortunately, of all the years, 2006 does not appear in Meherban's long list of K-2 expeditions. She says that both of them climbed to an altitude of 6,000 metres before they had to turn back.

Like all wives of HAPs, Gul Dana had spent a lot of sleepless nights while her husband was out there on the mountains. She would only feel relieved and delighted once he reappeared in the doorway safe and sound. She says that Jehan liked to spread his climbing gear in front of his three little children (two sons and one daughter), and would let them touch and examine one or the other piece.

In 2007, Jehan was once again on Gasherbrum-II with Meherban Shah. This is another expedition that Meherban did not mention.

In my conversation with Gul Dana, we have now come to the fatal year of 2008. Many Shimshalis believe in the predictive powers of dreams or misgivings. So does Gul Dana. She says that before her husband chose to go to the K-2 expedition, he had also received a call for Nanga Parbat. She tried to steer him towards the latter because whenever she thought of K-2, she was haunted by appalling notions and nightmares. However, she could not dissuade Jehan from going to the K-2 expedition because the mountain had always mesmerized him. In this respect, he did not differ from Hazil Shah, Amin Ullah Baig, Meherban Karim, and many others. He simply ignored that the odds on this giant mountain were as much against him as they were in his favour. He discounted the fact that the mountain of his dreams could also become the mountain of his death and did not realize that he might forever disappear on the icy heights of K-2.

Meherban Shah and Jehan Baig went together to this expedition. The oft-mentioned endlessly long period of bad weather dispirited all expedition members. Gul Dana says that the harmony in the two Shimshalis' group was suffering and deteriorating day by day. Eventually, an unbridgeable chasm gaped between the members on the one side and the HAPs on the other. The older Meherban Shah communicated the situation to the tour operator and was told to leave the group with Jehan and come back to Skardu.

At this point, Qudrat Ali suggested that Jehan should join Meherban Karim in order to help him and the Frenchman Hugues d'Aubarède with their summit bid. It sounded so simple and convincing. All preliminary work had been done, the route chalked out, ropes fixed, and the camps established. Jehan only had to 'walk up' and so he agreed. When Gul Dana learned of this, her nightmares almost suffocated her. Whatever little confidence she had preserved until now rapidly vanished and fear overwhelmed her. Without the much experienced Qudrat Ali, she saw her husband alongside the go-getter Meherban Karim, and the obstinate Frenchman, and with them she saw death walking.

Gul Dana thinks that her husband died while trying to save d'Aubarède's life. We do not know. He must have died high up in the region of camp 4. Jehan and Meherban's bodies were never found.

Since Jehan had accepted this job unofficially, the family's reimbursement was very modest. Both the mother and wife did not only lose a dear person, but also their livelihood. The children's education and future, which seemed secured by Jehan's HAP job, are now overshadowed by a lot of uncertainty.

Note

1. Prayer and assembly hall of the Ismaili community.

2.18

Farzar Khan

High-altitude porter, born 1950

FARZAR KHAN'S DARK, WEATHER-BEATEN FACE HAS BEEN engraved in my memory for many years. I meet him every summer because he is a member of Qudrat Ali's family. While I was living as a guest in Qudrat's house around 2003–04, 'Uncle' Farzar would occasionally show up. However, I did not have an inkling of his climbing record.

He is the second oldest of 'my' climbers after Rajab Shah. Unlike Rajab, he has not memorized the years of his expeditions. Instead, he opens the interview by rattling off the list of his mountains and the number of trips taken to each: twice to Nanga Parbat and K-2, four times to Gasherbrum-II, and once to Gasherbrum-I, Broad Peak, and Dhiran Peak. Towards the end of his climbing career, he scaled the five-thousand-metre peak Madele Sar with Meherban Shah and his nephew Qudrat.

Farzar Khan is the second of three brothers and two sisters. His late elder brother was Ali Musa's father.

When I bring up his schooling, I get a surprising response: he was never admitted to the first grade and I cannot help asking why. He replies that education at that time played a negligible role. I have to content myself with this answer.

To make up for it, he describes another game from his childhood in a graphic manner. The game is called *Ptuk*. It reminds me of badminton, the only difference being that there are no rackets. You use the soles of your feet instead, preferably jerking them up behind your back. The shuttlecock is made of an ordinary, but big button by threading as much long yak hair through its holes as possible. The hair is meant to give the button better flying ability.

Farzar stands up from the floor to demonstrate the technique of a *Ptuk* player. He tosses an imaginary button behind his back and hits it with the sole of his right foot. His agility and the speed of his movements remind me of a young football player presenting his mastery of the ball to marvelling spectators.

An integral part of his childhood memories is the annual migration to Pamir, the high pastures.

The year 1972 first took Farzar Khan out of Shimshal. He joined the Pakistan Army for a limited time in either Bunji or Janglot (near Gilgit). He quit the military service after six years because there was an extraordinary experience that made him seek his fortune elsewhere. It must have occurred in the summer of 1977 when, somewhere in his vicinity, a Czech film team was making an outdoor movie of sorts. He did not only witness this, but could make himself useful as an assistant in whatever little chore was required while the Europeans were drifting down the raging muddy Indus River to Chilas in rafts and shooting a movie of this nerve-rattling pastime. Farzar Khan was so impressed that he decided to leave the army and try his luck in tourism.

For the reader, it may no longer be a surprise. He set off on his first expedition without a trace of preliminary instruction. This was on Nanga Parbat with a Japanese team and the tour operator was Nazir Sabir. Farzar says they had reached camp 3 when the effort came to an abrupt end. A thunderstorm struck Nanga Parbat. At such extreme heights, human beings are in the very centre of the elements, as much exposed to them as they would be in the vent of an active volcano. Bent down as low as possible, one has to endure lightning and thunder pummelling the slopes and hope to be tiny enough not to be hit by lightning.

Not all of the members survived. One of the Japanese, who had not flung away his ice axe quickly enough, was killed by a bolt of lightning. Thereupon, the rest of the expedition was cancelled.

A year later, Farzar Khan was hired by a French group. Their destination was Gasherbrum-II. Tafat Shah was his colleague and both Shimshalis remember the leader of this expedition as a wealthy and generous individual. Farzar rummages in his documents and tracks down a visiting card, which, despite its tattered condition, is still perfectly readable. On it is the name of the prominent Frenchman, Monsieur Pierre Mazeaud. Later, when I went back to Germany, I found out that Monsieur Mazeaud used to be a French elite climber in the 1950s and, at the age of 48, summited Mount Everest in 1978 as the first French national to do so. His generosity was remarkably manifest on Gasherbrum-II when the expedition had to be cancelled because of unfavourable weather. Mazeaud declared that all the tents and equipment that the HAPs had laboriously hauled up to camp 3 were to be left behind without further ado.

Regardless of chronology, I ask Farzar Khan about his success on an eight-thousand-metre peak. Since I unexpectedly got a denial from a smiling Tafat Shah,[1] I have been prepared for surprises; however, Farzar can deliver, albeit without the year. We can work this out because he remembers that Qudrat Ali, in the same summer, stood on the summit of Nanga Parbat. Therefore, it must have been the year 2001.

Farzar Khan's eight-thousand-metre peak was Gasherbrum-II. He worked for a joint military expedition of the British and American armies. The leader was an American and, according to Farzar, an agreeable type. He is still thankful that this man, against the then rules, allowed him to participate in the summit bid. In the end, it was Ezat Ullah Baig, the American leader, and himself who stood on the highest point of Gasherbrum-II. All other members threw in the towel for various reasons.

Ezat Ullah's version of the story miraculously shares the year and the place with Farzar's; however, Ezat's group consisted of Greek climbers and not British and French soldiers.

I want to learn something about Farzar's K-2 experience. He names the expedition on which he cooperated with Amruddin—the joint venture between the Alpine Clubs of Pakistan and China. He also speaks of Captain Iqbal's devastating death. It is this last event which obliterates every other detail. He does not remember anything else.

About Broad Peak and all the other mountains on his list, I am unable to coax anything out of him; not even my most sophisticated questions help me here.

I ask myself what it is that could contribute towards giving the man an unmistakable profile. It could be his view of the HAPs' wages in Pakistan. Even on this, he does not utter a clear judgement. On the one hand, he says that his payment was not enough. On the other hand, it accorded him a step towards modest prosperity. Moreover, he says that one does not exclusively climb for money but also for fame and reputation.

His last expedition—the above-mentioned brief tour to Madele Sar that his nephew Qudrat Ali talked him into—

brought him such a splitting headache that he understood that it was a call from above for him to irrevocably turn his back on climbing.

As I inquire about his health, he has no complaints whatsoever, and he says that he is perfectly fine. In fact, year after year, I come across him while he's somewhere in the midst of hard physical work: digging a channel, rebuilding a wall, or planting poplar saplings on a slope high above the village. Farzar Khan does not shy away from any labour. As time has passed by, his cheeks appear to me increasingly hollowed.

Coming to the question of whether the younger generation should opt for an academic or a climbing career, his response is ambiguous. He says that he would definitely encourage youngsters to start climbing for the money and fame that comes along, but only if they feel that they are unable or don't want to advance their education.

What must be finally mentioned is Farzar Khan's role in the community of Shimshal. As early as 1971, he joined the Shimshal Volunteer Corps. After no less than thirty-six years of service, he retired in 2007 as Captain of Volunteers. He is still available for voluntary work if needed. After all, Farzar Khan is the epitome of a Shimshali.

Note

1. See Epilogue.

Epilogue

ON 19 MAY 2013, THE NEWS OF SAMINA BAIG SUMMITTING Mount Everest as the first Pakistani female to achieve this milestone came with a bang. Her achievement was celebrated for weeks, with the commencement of several events in her honour at all levels. She received substantial monetary gifts from the Government of Pakistan, the Aga Khan Foundation, and other institutions.

In 2008, I lived with Samina's family for four months. The family comprises her father Khyal Baig, mother Bibi Jaya, four elder brothers, and one sister. I have been well informed about the steps that led to the great event.

Mirza Ali, the youngest of Samina's brothers, joined me on several mountaineering tours around Shimshal. During our numerous conversations, I learned about his future plans and was also introduced to his personal philosophy of life. I was both impressed by the depth of his thought and puzzled by his overconfidence. However, in the following years, he pursued one of his aims with great endurance and did not allow himself to be diverted by any setback or mishap.

What was he focused on?

Mirza had envisioned two goals. First, he planned to promote women's rights in his country and, second, he wanted (and still wants) the unique Pakistani mountains to achieve reputation and popularity within Pakistan—something which has so far been denied to them. He founded Pakistan Youth Outreach in an attempt to attract Pakistan's women towards mountaineering. 'Gender equality' was the buzzword that he hoped would attract solidarity and interest in female mountaineering. The reader must remember that gender equality was also an issue in the third chapter *Climbing: A Job or a Philosophy*. Isn't it true that the Shimshal Mountaineering School is precisely pursuing this very goal? Why haven't Qudrat Ali and Shaheen Baig tried to win over the aspiring and idealistic Mirza for their project? Or should I instead ask why Mirza preferred to be a lone crusader in pursuing an objective that his fellow Shimshalis also espoused? A definite answer cannot be provided, and even though the absurdity is noticeable, we'll have to shrug our shoulders and try to ignore it. In Pakistan's climbing stronghold, Shimshal, there are two factions which have the same ambition but ignore each other, not to mention that they compete with each other.

Public attention and interest in Mirza's organization, Pakistan Youth Outreach, had remained negligible. Although the idea of gender equality still doesn't kindle much interest in Pakistani society, the likes of Mirza refuse to give up. As someone who has an intelligent, ambitious, and self-confident younger sister, Mirza decided that he would make her a brilliant example of his ideas.

After the siblings had done a few smaller climbs in Pakistan, Mirza focused on the world's highest mountain, Mount Everest—also because the year 2013 marked the 60th anniversary of Everest's first climb. Mirza has a magic touch for winning sponsors so the siblings indeed started for Everest and, like hundreds of others, updated the world online on an almost daily basis. Everything went according to the plan.

For 19 May, a window of good weather was forecast. Mirza wanted to make it to the summit without using supplementary oxygen—a goal that was not realized. However, Samina used bottled oxygen and was among the 146 climbers who stood atop the peak of Mount Everest on this memorable day.

Samina's achievement pleases Shimshalis greatly. The name of their village has been carried across the world and their reputation as excellent climbers has been established in a spectacular fashion.

***

Tafat Shah is one man who appears in the epilogue because he does not meet my criterion of being the climber of an eight-thousander. Shimshalis regard Tafat as the pioneer of high-altitude climbing in their village. Samad and I interviewed him because we were absolutely convinced that he must have summited at least one eight-thousander. However, we were nonplussed when he denied this.

Tafat Shah was born around 1957 and started high-altitude portering at a very early age, even before Rajab Shah. He is said to be the most skilled and bravest of the Shimshali HAPs. The first climb of Mingli Sar is ascribed to Tafat Shah,[1] before Nazir Sabir—often named as Mingli's pioneer climber—came along. Besides the typical tours, he has climbed Tirich Mir (7,708m in the Hindu Kush), and also the extremely difficult Ultar Peak (7,388m). On the latter, he was with a Japanese team. It took them three attempts to make it to the top, Tafat Shah being denied the summit by the Japanese.

Even though Tafat has never seen a school from the inside, he is a politically conscious citizen and a staunch supporter of the Pakistan Peoples Party (PPP). A PPP poster is pasted on the front door of his house. In the family room, he has hung a life-size portrait of Benazir Bhutto, taken minutes before her assassination.

We also have a lengthy discussion with him about the strange rift between the SMS and the siblings, Mirza Ali and Samina Baig. He regrets that they have not been able to cooperate and outlines some reasons for it. Qudrat and Shaheen, who could choose between a profitable job with an oil company and the less rewarding occupation of climbing in their native village, may have preferred the former and forsaken the latter. Mirza may have refrained from cooperation due to his individualism and high-handedness. For Tafat Shah, it is a pity that the huge potential for synergy has been forfeited in Shimshal.

***

Five eight-thousander summiteers remain without a text of their own. All my efforts to interview them ended in futility. Shaheen Baig and Qudrat Ali are introduced in the fifth chapter. Whereas Qudrat's climbing record is included in my book about his wife Lal Paree, I deeply regret that in the course of two summer seasons, I was unable to get hold of his friend Shaheen Baig. He is a truly great climber and should have been granted a chapter in this book. However, it exceeded my means and possibilities to trace him.

Other than them, Samad and I had to chase three more climbers as well. We made appointments which were not kept. Many a time, we were turned back from the front door and eventually grew tired of it. If Faizal Ali, Wahab Ali Shah, and Sajjad Karim are not interested in a chapter of their own, so be it.

In the summer of 2013, I visited a handful of high-altitude porters who had just returned from their eight-thousander expeditions, in order to update my record. The first of them was Amin Ullah Baig. He had been on Broad Peak with eleven Germans and Austrians. None of the climbers had reached the top, but they managed to ascend to a secondary point called 'rocky summit'.

In the middle of the expedition routine, on 23 June, the news about the massacre of foreign climbers at the base camp of Nanga Parbat burst in. There was shock and horror at the incomprehensible act. But the attack did not have much impact on life at the other base camps for there is a decisive difference between Nanga Parbat and the rest of the eight-thousanders. While the former is not far from KKH and thus easy to reach, the remoteness of the others means that a similar terror attack would be a lot harder to carry out and is therefore rather improbable. There was, however, a different effect to observe: the phone calls which the climbers received via satellite from their family and relatives back home. It required a lot of placating and reassuring to assuage the fears of the families. Mothers and wives beseeched their loved ones to pack up and run but to no avail. Nobody left the base camps of K-2, Broad Peak, and the Gasherbrums. Still, Amin expects that the frail entity of mountain tourism in Pakistan, vulnerable as it has always been, will have to suffer a new wave of setbacks, which will in turn ruin the hopes of the high-altitude porters.

I ask him about his latest winter expedition with the Poles. Three-and-a-half months in the freezing exile, far from the comfort and warmth of his family and friends, the deaths of two people, all this is no headache to him. It is not only the better payment that keeps attracting him; the other reason is that summiting an eight-thousander in winter counts a lot more than doing so in the warm season. He wishes to make a name for himself. With a sigh, I try to understand his viewpoint.

This year, the HAPs received 2,500 rupees per day—a minimal increase in relation to the relentless inflation in Pakistan.

Farhad Khan, whom I visited next, was Amin Ullah Baig's colleague on the German-Austrian Broad Peak expedition. He praises the members' commitment. He felt fine with them. His information on the wages is different from Amin's. He tells me that they were paid 2,000 rupees per day.

Then he rummages around a bit and gets hold of two small airtight plastic containers. He scatters the content before my eyes and asks me to explain it.

What I see is an assortment of tablets and ampoules plus syringes—carefully portioned, labelled, and packed. It is probably some life-saving ration for each high camp— dexamethasone and nifedipine against high-altitude pulmonary and cerebral oedema, one extremely strong painkiller in case of severe injuries, and a lot of high-dosage ibuprofen. I am able to explain to him the purpose and application of these medicines, which he obviously inherited from the expedition members. All expeditions end in this gift-giving ritual: the HAPs receive surplus foods, instant coffee, chocolate spreads, peanut butter, and energy bars. Mostly, they also get well-preserved equipment items such as gloves, protective sunglasses, and fleece jackets. Yet, to give away highly efficient prescription drugs to the high-altitude porters, who do not understand what they are for is slightly discomfiting. I put the stuff back in the boxes, hoping that they will never be reopened.

★★★

Sarwar Ali was on Broad Peak in July and August of 2013 and, briefly, on K-2. Along with a high-altitude porter from Baltistan, he worked for a woman from Mongolia who, according to him, is her country's best female mountaineer, and after summiting Mount Everest (with supplementary oxygen) has the vision of climbing all fourteen eight-thousanders.

She did not make it to the summit of Broad Peak, which might partly be due to the shock she suffered from the calamity of another expedition.

Three climbers of an Iranian team had reached the highest point of Broad Peak and had thereupon started their descent, but on the opposite side, for inexplicable reasons. They seemed to have lost all sense of direction and stumbled into increasingly difficult terrain until they were totally stranded. They sent several radio messages to the base camp. Their companions understood how hopeless their situation had become, all the more since in their disorientation they had started to retrace their steps towards the summit.

The last radio contact came from an altitude of about 7,200 metres. In this area, all three of them must have run out of their last bit of energy and consciousness and subsequently fell to their deaths.

Sarwar Ali's team was also making a summit bid at this moment, but after hearing the unfortunate news, the Mongolian and the Balti HAP cancelled their attempt. Sarwar carried on in the hope that he would be able to rescue someone. He was appalled to discover that the footprints of the three men were heading towards virtually inaccessible terrain.

While he was trying to approach the casualties, he heard the rattle of a helicopter. It had been alerted by the base camp, but was too late for a rescue. Moreover, the photos taken by the helicopter crew of the accident site clearly proved that the terrain would never have allowed any rescue or recovery operation. On his radio, Sarwar received a request that he must give up his attempt and descend.

He feels that his success on Broad Peak is overshadowed. However, for his selfless devotion, the Iranians' expedition leader wrote him an appreciative certificate (see photograph).

After Broad Peak, the Mongolian climber wished to explore K-2 for the purpose of a future climb. The trip was terminated at camp 1. In mid-August, Sarwar Ali was back home in Shimshal.

***

In retrospect, I find one story to be quite doubtful: the 1997 Everest expedition with Rajab Shah and Meherban Shah. I met two gentlemen who, independent of each other, called themselves good friends of Nazir Sabir's. The first, Karim Hayat (tour operator, Mountains Expert), knows one more reason other than that assumed by Rajab and Meherban for why the summit bid was called off. The people, i.e. all except Nazir Sabir, had polished off all edibles while ascending to the highest camp and had therefore provoked the failure. My other source of information is a movie maker from Islamabad, whose name I forgot to ask in our brief encounter. He had heard of 'three' summit bids, which is evidence that Nazir Sabir can in no way be blamed for the weakness. Moreover, he argues that Colonel Sher Khan would never have accepted an order for retreat without good reason. According to him, it was the relentless high-altitude gales that thwarted everything in the end.

***

The sponsor of the SMS girls' team, Sherbano Saiyid, remained silent and unseen in the summer of 2013.

In the same year, certain events transpired in an unexpected fashion. The AKRSP, in cooperation with a six-member delegation of experienced climbers from Italy and two Afghan climbing professionals, invited some thirty young people from across Gojal to Passu for a 17-day training camp. Eight men and four women were summoned from Shimshal, including Amin Ullah Baig. The location was the classy Sarai Hotel by the glacier, with quick access to the training grounds (further confirming Ali Musa's assertion that the SMS is located in the wrong place).

For theoretical climbing instruction, the coaches had brought laptops, screens, and beamers, and thus established the high standard of the event. At the end of the training camp, each of the participants was given a certificate granting them non-official titles, such as 'Trekking Guide' or 'Instructor'. Recalling Ali Musa's sceptical remarks about the alleged lack of perspective among young women, who according to him 'undertake climbing just for fun', I asked the elder brother of one of the girls and quoted Ali Musa's pessimistic phrase. Javed Raheem rejected this view.

'Of course the girls could now work as guides for trekking groups,' he said.

This sounded new to my ears. I needed to be sure. I told him to envision a situation where a group of Italian or French mountaineers (say five males and one female), would want to hire his sister for a tour to the Spantik base camp, and then asked if his father would agree.

To this, he instantly responded in the affirmative. If there is something palpably shifting towards gender equality in Pakistan's remotest mountain villages, I wish for it in the girls' best interest. Their self-confidence has clearly been boosted by their latest achievements. However, they would need to do a crash course in English (custom-made for trekking routine). This shortcoming is still a big obstacle.

***

In the summer of 2013, I witnessed a new phenomenon. Young Shimshalis in growing numbers are getting fond of picnics that generally entail mountain tours or other forms of trekking for a duration of several days. In the previous year, I had still considered it an extremely rare thing (see the third chapter), but it definitely seems to have taken root now. This means that Shimshalis are now engaging in mountaineering for fun and excitement. It is good to see groups of class fellows or friends (sexes strictly separated), and also young married couples, setting off with mattresses and sleeping bags to spend a night in a shepherds' house high up in the pastures just for the sake of it, without a mission to fulfil, or a burden to carry.

On my two visits to the high pasture Shuwerth in 2013, I noted another step into an uncertain future. Shimshalis appear to have forgotten a basic rule: the yaks must by all means be kept outside the winter pastures on the banks of the Baraldu River. In their hundreds, they were grazing in Chikor and Goskhun and in this way robbed themselves of their winter fodder. Not long ago, this was regarded as a disaster. There were a few efforts to chase them away and back up to Shuwerth, which remained quite ineffectual single actions. When I asked whether the community council could not stop this ominous development, I earned a shrug of the shoulders. The fact of the matter is that there are not enough people who are able and willing to spend their summers up there and tend to the yaks. What can a community council do against it? To prevent the worst—yak babies starving to death in winter or falling prey to wolves and snow leopards—some families have started to take them down to the village and feed them there. Of four-hundred yak babies, some two-hundred and fifty come to Shimshal for the winter.

***

On 18 April 2014, a disaster took place on Mount Everest, the gravity of which makes for a sorry record on the world's highest mountain. Sixteen people were killed by an avalanche between base camp and camp 1. The victims were all Sherpas, who were preparing the route with fixed ropes and ladders for the hordes of paying clients who invade Everest year after year.

***

Two new events, which complete the picture of Shimshali ambitions and achievements, have to be noted here.

On 26 July 2014, three Shimshalis stood on the summit of K-2. They had joined a Pakistani-Italian expedition to mark the 60th anniversary of K-2's first climb in 1954.

Amin Ullah Baig and Faizal Ali had worked as high-altitude porters and Rehmat Ullah Baig had been a member of this joint expedition. I am sure the reader remembers Amin Ullah Baig's dream, which has now come true.

The siblings, Samina Baig and Mirza Ali, set an entirely new Pakistani record of ascending the 'Seven Summits'.[1] To stand atop the highest peaks of each continent, including Mt Vinson (4,892m) in Antarctica, has been an attraction for climbers since the 1950s. The milestone was first achieved in 1985 by the Americans Richard Bass and Frank Wells.

The brother and sister duo of Mirza Ali and Samina Baig have now become models of initiative and courage in Pakistan.

To everybody's dismay, Rajab Shah passed away on 30 April 2015 at the age of 66. He was Shimshal's greatest climber and a pillar of the community at large. Shimshal will not be the same without him. May God rest his soul in peace.

In the end, I would like to extend my gratitude to Joan Faith Mey, who proofread the manuscript and polished my English.

Leutkirch, Germany
15 April 2017

Notes

1. This is denied by others.
2. The highest peaks of the seven continents.

P.S. Ever since the research for this book was completed in 2015, Shimshal has seen some infrastructural and technological advancement. The remote village in Pakistan is no more alien to internet and mobile phone service. There might have been some more summit successes that the author has not been able to mention as she can no longer travel to Shimshal.

Bibliography

Bowley, Graham, 2010, *No Way Down*, London, Harper Collins.

Fladt, Christiane, 2010, *Wenn Allah nein sagt*, Jena, Verlag Neue Literatur.

Hopkirk, Peter, 1990, *The Great Game*, London, published by John Murray.

Kammerlander, Hans, 2012, *Zurück nach Morgen*, München, Piper Malik.

Kropp, Göran, 1998, *Allein auf den Everest*, München, Goldmann Publishing Company.

Lücker, Walter, 2013, *Der höchste Berg*, München, Piper Malik.

Mock, John & O'Neill, Kimberley, 2002, *Trekking in the Karakoram and Hindukush*, Melbourne, Oakland, London, Paris, Lonely Planet Publications.

Thapa, Deepak, 2008, 'Viel versprechende Zukunft für nepalesische Bergsteiger?' In *Reise in den Himalaya*, ed. Alice Grünfelder, Zürich, Unionsverlag.